AND HE TOLD THEM A STORY

Background on Luke's Parables

Richard Carl Hoefler

AND HE TOLD THEM A STORY

ISBN 0-89536-383-6

PRINTED IN U.S.A.

TABLE OF CONTENTS

Introduction

This is the first volume of a two-volume work on the parables used in the Three Year Cycle of the Church Year. This volume deals with the eleven parables from Luke.

Jesus told parables to his people that they might better understand his message and mission. He also told parables to people considered his enemies. Some scholars have called this use of parables "weapons of warfare." But it is better thought of as a surgical use of the parables. The cutting, knife-like edge is still there but its intention is not to destroy and kill but to correct and cure.

Today the parables are more than likely some of the most popular passages of scripture. They appeal to people because they are stories, and everybody likes to hear a good story. However, a parable is more than just a good story; it is a metaphor which is a figure of speech in which the similarity of one object or action to another is implied. Metaphor literally means "future talk." And that is what the parables of Jesus are. They are stories meant to open up new visions of reality, new insights into spirituality, and new options for human potentiality.

The parables invite both friends and enemies of Jesus into a story, to become involved in that story, participate in it, and ultimately be changed by it.

The chapters of this book are not sermons, but discussions based on classroom lectures concerned with presenting the preaching values of the parables. Ideas from scholars are presented together with illustrations and suggestions intended to provide preachers and teachers the material necessary for the construction of sermons and lectures on the parables in Luke.

A sermon is what happens when a text is brought into contact with life. The Word makes contact with the world and a spark ignites. That spark is the basis for a sermon. For each person this contact point and spark may be different, as the experiences of people are different. And for the same person sparks may occur at different points of contact when situations change. Therefore, this book is designed to create "live ends" of the Word and the world in the hope that as they are brought together in the reader's mind the needed spark for a sermon will occur.

Parable Interpretation

For more than a thousand years the parables were interpreted as allegory. Each detail of the story was viewed as a miniature vault wherein spiritual mysteries were stored. In 1910 Juelicher singlehandedly destroyed the allegorical method. He maintained that the intention of the parables was to prove or convince and since only one thing could be proved at a time the parable could have only one single point. For Julicher this was a neat little moral teaching. The popular expression of this approach was given in the definition of a parable as an "earthly example of a heavenly truth."

The most influential work on the parables was done by the historical critics. Cadoux of Glasgow (1931) paved the way for this approach to the parables, but it was C. H. Dodd of Oxford (1935) and his German contemporary Joachim Jeremias (1947) who brought the interpreters of the parables an awareness of the change the parables underwent as they moved from an oral tradition to a written form. They pointed out the decisive difference between **tradition,** what the parables meant when Jesus first used them, and **redaction,** how the Early Church and the writers of the gospels used the parables in their accounts. The parables were now seen not as neat little moral truths, but as weapons of warfare Jesus used to attack his enemies and as exhortations to the church to adjust to changing conditions. The main concern was to discover the historical setting in which the parables were used.

This historical interpretation dominated the academic world of parable interpretation until about ten years ago when two new approaches were suggested by Narrative Theology and Structural Exegesis.

Narrative Theology and Structural Exegesis are both reactions to the schools of historical criticism. Their intention is not to destroy or detract from the contributions made by the historical critics, but to add another dimension or consideration to the hermeneutical process. As mentioned above, this century has been dominated by the historical method. The problem was to move behind the biblical record to the event itself. The task was to identify within the scriptures what were the original words of Jesus and what were the additions and changes made by the Early Church.

Redaction Criticism begins with the author and attempts to establish his intentionality. He had a purpose for his writing and this determined the way in which he selected, organized and presented his materials. Literary Criticism went a step further to examine the sources used by the writers to see how they reflected a previous purpose of the Early Church as they adapted the materials of oral tradition to fit their particular situation, such as the delayed coming of Jesus, the influx of Gentiles into the Church and the moral needs of practicing Christianity in a pagan world. Form Criticism attempted to get back to the original oral tradition and see how the accounts of Our Lord's life and his teachings were used in worship, education and evangelism.

Now in each case the criterion was history. A research of the materials of scriptures was done to establish the facts, what Jesus said in the first place and how these materials were changed and adjusted to fit particular needs. Now Narrative Theology and Structural

Exegesis are both reactions against what they consider to be an over-emphasis on the historical. They take the position that in the process of discovering the facts of revelation the inner meaning of the texts themselves has been slighted. The historical approach has been so concerned with what Jesus actually said and what the Church did with what he said, that they have failed to do justice to the full meaning of what he said. So rather than being concerned with the author or the historical setting and use of the text, Narrative Theology and Structural Exegesis have focused in on the text itself. They view the text as story — as an account which possesses in and of itself an integrity. And as text alone they have examined it from a literary point of view to discover the meaning which it possesses as a story.

The basic difference between the historical critics and the Narrative-Structural critics is that the historical critics look through the text to something else — namely the setting or situation outside the text. By relating the parable to this outside material which surrounded it, the meaning of the parable could be established. The Narrative-Structural interpreters look at the text itself. The form and the relationship of the various elements within the story determined its meaning or meanings.

In the discussions of the parables which follow, both the interpretation of the historical critics and the Narrative-Structural critics will be used because both enlighten the total impact of the parables. The parables will be viewed, however, primarily as story. But they are stories which can be understood only as related to two other primary stories.

There are three stories that concern us in the treatment of parables that follows. First there is the story of the parable itself. Here the interpretation of Narrative Theology and Structural Exegesis will be of great help. Secondly there is the larger story told by the Bible itself in which the parable is imbedded. Here the historical critics will be informative. The third story is the story of the listeners. Each person who hears a parable has a life story of his own. He has had certain experiences which have created problems, established ideas and opinions, and developed habitual reactions. The task of parable interpretation is to place the story of the parable alongside both of the other two stories.

First the story of the parable is placed alongside the total story of the Bible. The Creation, Fall, Covenant, Law, Prophets, the life of Jesus and the writings of Paul are seen as the background in which the parables were told. The parables seldom introduce new revelations, but in each case they dramatize an aspect of the total story. It is not always necessary that the original teller of the parable was aware of this relationship. For example, in the Parable of the Soils it is not absolutely necessary that Jesus had the optimism of God in mind when he told the parable. If, when the parable is placed over against the total revelation of Scripture, the interpreter sees this biblically revealed optimism of God dramatized in the story the parable tells, then it is legitimate if the spark for the sermon occurs at this point. The parable as story is a dynamic Word of God and if when placed in contact with the Bible story a spark occurs and a relationship is seen, this can be an acceptable basis for a sermon.

In the same manner, when you place the story of the parable alongside the life stories of the listeners, certain relationships will emerge. They may not have been in the mind of the original teller of the story but they are legitimate if the parable honestly speaks to this experience in the life of the listener.

The parables as story have an integrity in and of themselves. As most scholars agree they represent some of the most original and reliable materials of the Gospels. Here more than anywhere else in the New Testament we have words actually spoken by Jesus. The parables are not therefore secondary materials which simply illustrate the Bible story, but are a vital part of that revelation. As the Word of God they are dynamic and not static. They are not nuts which have to be cracked to find within them the static truth previously placed there by Jesus. With the rest of scripture they are living words spoken by God and when brought into contact with the listeners can convey ever fresh new understandings of God's will for us today.

Some readers may feel that the method suggested by the comparative relationship of the three stories is a return to a form of allegorization. However, this is not the case. Allegorization is finding within each detail of the story a hidden comparative relationship. Each character and object has its corresponding reality in life. The method in this discussion of the parables is that of "plot parallelism." The parables are viewed basically as dramas in which the action in most cases is more important than the characters or the object involved. The parables are stories in which the similarity of one action to another action is implied. We see in the plot of the parable a dramatization of actions within the story of the Bible and within our own experiences.

The important thing, therefore, is not that the parables are stories with one point, but that they are stories with a plot. It is the plot of the parable that is the key to interpretation. When this plot is placed alongside the story of the Bible and the story of our lives, the meaning and the message of the parables emerge for our time.

Salvation
Of
A
Shady
Lady

1

THE PARABLE OF THE TWO DEBTORS
Luke 7:36-50

In small Southern towns, after the sermon on Sunday Morning it is customary to invite the preacher and his family over for a dinner of fried chicken, rice, and gravy. A similar occasion is the setting of the Parable of the Two Debtors. Luke does not mention the fact but it is safe to assume that Jesus had preached that day, perhaps in the local synagogue. After the service Simon invited him home for dinner. It may have been that the Pharisee was just curious about this young prophet from Nazareth and wanted to learn more about him. Or Simon may have had in mind to test him. This is suggested by the statement he makes later on in the text, "If this man really were a prophet, he would know who this woman is who is touching him." But whatever Simon's reason might have been, Jesus accepts the invitation.

As they are reclining about the table, a woman walks up to Jesus apparently to thank him for his sermon. She had been greatly impressed with the words of this new prophet. For the first time in her life she had heard about God's love and willingness to forgive sinners. She was well aware of what she had become, as were most of the people in the village. She had sold her body to every man willing to pay the price, and she was becoming aware that with each sale she was losing more and more of her self-respect. Then hearing that God loved her despite her sinful ways, she was overcome with amazement and gratitude that God could accept her even when she could no longer accept herself. This unmerited love of God's grace and forgiveness had worked a change in her, and she felt as if she were a new person.

She was so grateful that she had to seek out the man who had done this for her, and thank him personally. But when she saw him her emotions got the better of her. Unable to restrain herself, she burst into tears and began kissing and washing his feet with her tears and wiping them with her hair.

She was not an invited guest at the dinner, but it was customary for friends of those invited to seek them out at dinner parties when they wanted to talk with them. In fact, the host provided cushions arranged around the edge of the room where people could wait for an opportunity, like a lull in the conversation at the table, to go up and speak with the person they wanted to see.

Simon, in this day long before women's lib, might have been surprised with the entry of any woman into the main room of a house where guests were present, except for the purpose of serving the meal, for it was not the usual sight. What really shocked Simon was not the fact that a woman had crashed the party, but her uncontrollable display of emotions. Wallace[1] sees in this aspect of the account a glaring contrast between the woman and Simon. The response of the woman was a warm, free, spontaneous expression of adoration. Simon, on the other hand, was cold and almost indifferent to Jesus. He provided no water to wash his feet. He gave him no kiss of welcome and friendship. Now this does not necessarily mean that Simon had singled Jesus out to insult him publicly. Rather, it reveals the character of Simon as a person. He was not a warm outgoing type of person. Hunter refers to him as "pious prissy Simon."[2] This might be a little strong, but all the evidence of the story suggests that he was indifferent and unresponsive to other people. He lived in his own superior, self-centered world. He was the perfect example of a person with a "holier-than-thou" attitude. When he did react to other people it was to judge them as being inferior to him.

Simon could very well have been the Pharisee who stood in the Temple and prayed, "God, I thank thee that I am not like other men."

Simon was doubly shocked, for he recognized the emotional woman was not just an ordinary woman, which would have been bad enough, but she was the notorious local prostitute, the shady lady of the village. Then to top it off Simon was actually horrified to see Jesus calmly accept what she was doing to him and take no offense at it. That was more than Simon could take. He thinks to himself, "If this man really were a prophet, he would know who this woman is who is **touching** him; he would know what kind of a sinful life she leads!" Bailey[3] points out that the Greek word used here for "touching" also means "to light a fire" and carries with it sexual connotations. Granted, it is the feet of Jesus that were being touched, but in the mind of Simon the whole affair was a highly improper scene. She is a sinner and everybody knows this, so Jesus should have nothing to do with her. Even an ordinary woman would hesitate to publicly speak to a rabbi; to see a woman with her reputation touch him was absolutely indecent.

Jesus is aware that Simon is upset and so he turns to him and gently says, "Simon, I have something to tell you." "Yes, Teacher," he says, "tell me." Then Jesus tells the story of the two debtors. One owed a great debt and the other a small one. Both are forgiven. Then Jesus asks Simon, "Which one, then, will love him more?" Simon answers, "I suppose that it would be the one who was forgiven more." Jesus responds, "Your answer is correct." Then follows a very profound insight into human nature and faith. Jesus shows that even though Simon knows the right answer, he himself is not right. His religion is in his head but not in his heart.

I remember when I first began to teach, one of my professors gave me sound advice. He said, "When a student gives a wrong response to your question, never say to him, 'You are wrong.' Rather say, 'Your answer is wrong.' " There is a vital difference between giving wrong answers and being wrong as a person. In one case you are making a judgment concerning the nature of a person. In the other, you are only evaluating an idea. And the converse of this applies to Jesus' treatment of Simon. He says, "Your answer is correct. You have the right idea." But then he goes on to point out that Simon as a person is **not** correct. He is wrong. Jesus shows Simon that he is cold, aloof, superior and indifferent in his treatment of others because there is no love in his heart. Simon was patronizing Jesus, showing condescension by neglecting the ordinary attentions paid by a host to guests of his own rank. It should be noted that the custom of foot washing was not an absolute rule of social etiquette. But it was a common expression of warm hospitality and friendly love.

Jesus points this out to Simon by stressing the contrast between the conduct of the woman and that of Simon toward himself. The woman was loving and kind because she had experienced God's great love and forgiveness. Simon, on the other hand, was a stranger to God's love. He had an intellectual association with God but not a personal one. He was quite satisfied with his own righteousness and thus experienced no forgiveness which might have made real for him, in a personal way, the mercy of God. Consequently in his personal relationship with people he exhibited little or no love.

Simon represented the people who caused Christ the greatest trouble in his ministry: people who were so well established in their state of righteousness that their ears were closed to the words Christ had to speak; people who were so zealous in the right keeping of the Law that they were no longer conscious of their own sins.

In his sermon on this text, Henry Ward Beecher[4] points out that a serious sense of sin is not so much a requirement for entering into a relationship with God as it is the result of it. To stand in the presence of God is to be truly aware of one's sins. God's holiness reveals our true sinfulness. But for Simon this was not so. He was so concerned with his own self-righteousness that he had lost all sensitivity to guilt. Jesus says to him, "Simon, you are wrong. This woman is better than you, for she has experienced great forgiveness and therefore she is able to express great love to God and to others."

Christ Is The Problem

So often we hear the pious platitude that Christ is the answer, as if once Christ entered our lives, suddenly — no more problems. However, the opposite is true. In the state of our natural sinfulness we could be quite happy sinners. Then when Christ enters in and disturbs us we become aware of and sensitive to the fact that we are sinful. Simon was a contented man, completely satisfied with his life until he invited Jesus home for dinner; then things were never quite the same.

So for us. I can go to church and feel very good about reaching down in my pocket and putting a dollar bill on the offering plate. But Christ leans over my shoulder and says, "Now wait a minute, you can afford to give more than that." I can sit down at a table loaded with delicious and appetizing food and take it all for granted as part of the bountiful life we assume is ours. Then Christ reminds me of the thousands of starving children in the world. I can drive casually by a hospital in my sinful state of indifference. Then Christ rolls down the window of my car and reminds me of the lonely and troubled people in that hospital who desperately need to be visited. Christ becomes my problem. He makes me constantly aware of my wrongdoings and shortcomings.

Christ is not the answer to our problems. He **is** our problem. The closer we come to him the more sensitive we become to our own sinfulness. Simon experienced this in his encounter with Christ. He invited Jesus home to dinner to size him up. But Simon soon discovered that it was not he who was evaluating Jesus, it was Jesus who was evaluating him. And Simon found himself wanting.

New Definition Of Morality

Granskou[5] says that this parable turns the tables on the Pharisees. They thought that they were the most moral of all, but they had actually lost their morality through respectability. If morality means love for others, then the Pharisees were immoral men. They were so satisfied with their fulfillment of the Law that they felt no guilt, and, feeling no guilt, they had failed to experience forgiveness which would have made of them moral men.

Simon had judged the woman to be immoral because of her sins. Jesus says she is moral because her deeds of love reveal her morality. It is her forgiveness that makes of her a moral person. This turns upside-down the common view of morality based on doing the good works of the Law and abstaining from doing what the Law forbids. A person is made moral by God's forgiveness and because of this a person does good deeds. It is not good deeds that make us moral persons; it is the moral person who does good deeds.

Christ further presents the irony of moral people who lose their morality through respectability. They become so respectable that they no longer feel the need of forgiveness and when that happens they become immoral persons. To be a truly moral person is to reside in a continuous state of being forgiven.

The Anonymous Woman

Scholars have been concerned with this woman's identity. Just who was this shady lady? There are three possiblities. She could have been Mary Magdalene, which means Mary from the town of Magdala in Galilee. From her dominant role in the New Testament, the English word has been coined — "magdalen" — which the dictionary defines as a "reformed prostitute." The similarity of profession might suggest they were the same person. However, Francis L. Filas in his book **The Parables of Jesus**[6] comes to the conclusion that the shady lady of our account was not Mary Magdalene, because in the eighth chapter of Luke which follows this account Mary Magdalene is introduced as if for the first time.

Mary of Bethany, the sister of Martha and Lazarus, is a second possibility. But Filas finds it even more difficult to identify the woman with Mary of Bethany, for the time and place are all wrong. Bethany is one hundred miles south of Capernaum where our story takes place. Also, the time is wrong as the anointing account at Bethany took place six days before Jesus died, whereas our story happened at least a year earlier.

This issue is more complicated by the fact that some scholars, particularly in the West since the time of Gregory the Great, believe Mary Magdalene and Mary of Bethany were the same person. Matthew (25:6-13), Mark (14:3-9), and John (12:1-8) all record the account of an anointing at Bethany where a woman broke an alabaster flask of very costly oil and anointed Jesus. John identifies this woman as Mary the sister of Lazarus. Matthew and Mark do not. All agree that this happened in the house of Simon the Leper. Our story occurs in the house of Simon the Pharisee. The general opionion of biblical scholars today is that this is not the same event but two different anointings and that the two Marys are not the same person.

The third possibility is that the shady lady of our story was neither Mary Magdalene nor Mary of Bethany but simply an anonymous woman whose dramatic interruption of Simon's dinner provided the setting for the Parable of the Two Debtors. Her identity is not important. It is what she did that will be remembered both by Simon the Pharisee and by us.

However, so far as the preaching values of this account are concerned, it is important that even though the woman remains nameless this in no way should imply that she was a nobody. In the sight of Jesus she was an important somebody. She was a person and not just another prostitute. Jesus makes this quite clear when he says to Simon, "Do you see this woman?" This is precisely Simon's problem. He could not see this woman as a person; he simply classified her as a prostitute, therefore could see no good in her.

Is this not our problem? We classify people into closed little categories. As the nursery rhyme goes, "Rich man, poor man, beggar man, thief." We see a black man, a Chink, a Dego and we remark, "They all look alike to me." In this text Christ is warning us not to categorize people and put labels on them, but to see them as persons.

Christ sees this woman not as a sinner because she has broken the law and lives an immoral life; he sees her as a child of God. That which motivated him was not just her lostness but more important her belongingness. Jesus associated with sinners because they were separated from God. His concern was not to reform but to restore a person to a right relationship to God. He viewed all persons as potentially good because they belonged to God. The shepherd searched for **his** sheep. The lady swept the house looking for **her** coin. The father loved the prodigal and welcomed him home because he was **his** son.

The way we look at sinners makes all the difference in our approach toward them. We are to see them as lost brothers, not as sinning strangers. A little child once did a terrible thing and a man observing the situation said to the father of the boy, "If he were my son, I would beat him within an inch of his life." To which the father replied, "I would, too, if he were your son."

Jesus came not as a social reformer attacking prostitution, crime and moral corruption. He came as a savior of people. They were sinners in our Lord's sight not because they were doing wrong and immoral things, but because their state of sinfulness was separating them from God. That is why he did not condemn persons but freed them from their sins so that they could return home. Christ never lectured to the sinners but liberated them from their sins.

Simon looked at the woman and saw only the sinful life she was leading. Christ looked at the woman and saw the person she could bcome.

Penitent Or Grateful

Many interpreters view the actions of the woman as penitential. Having heard that Jesus could forgive sins, she comes begging for his mercy in the only way that she knows how. She washes his feet with her tears of repentance, kisses them and pours the oil of remorse upon them. However, the story does not support such a penitential approach. It does not say that she came and knelt before him begging his forgiveness, nor does she prostrate herself confessing her sinful life. Rather the text says, "She stood behind Jesus by his feet, crying and wetting his feet with her tears." This is not the posture of penitence, and these are not tears of remorse seeking forgiveness. This is the posture of gratitude, and these are the tears of joy. She is responding to what she has received, not attempting to win something more. This woman has been forgiven and she is expressing spontaneous thankfulness.

Jesus makes this clear when he points out to Simon that he failed to wash his feet and welcome him with a kiss. Simon was ungrateful in his hospitality to Jesus for he owed Jesus nothing. He was, in his own mind, doing

Jesus a favor by simply inviting him into his house for dinner. But this woman had come to Jesus overflowing with love and gratitude. She had shown him true hospitality by washing and kissing his feet and anointing his head. He had done a great thing for her, and she could not hold back the emotional expression of her profound gratitude.

Simple Salvation

It is also interesting to note that even though this is a story about the salvation of a shady lady, there is no mention of the word salvation. Straton[7] points out that there is no evidence that she came seeking salvation. There is no account of her confession. She was not a student of the scriptures. She certainly knew no theology about how God could forgive sins through Christ. All she was aware of was her great need, and Christ's willingness to forgive her and to give her a second chance to live again. She had undoubtedly heard the word Christ preached. But nothing more.

How often we make the whole process of salvation too complex with elaborate procedural methods and rituals of confession and penitence. Salvation becomes a formal theological discipline. But here the baggage of centuries of dogmatic argument is torn away and we see only the simple story of salvation. A woman aware of her great need hears the story of God's love for sinners through Christ, and she turns her back on her old way of living and learns to love others. Salvation is as decisively simple and as simply decisive as that.

Justification By Faith

Within this incident we see preshadowed Paul's teaching of justification by faith through grace. The woman is forgiven by grace and not by any merit of her own. She has been forgiven; what follows is an outpouring of love and gratitude because she has experienced the unmerited mercy of God.

This is sometimes missed because the King James version states, verse 47, "Wherefore I say unto thee, her sins, which are many, are forgiven; **for** she loved much." This would imply that she was forgiven because she loved much. Her loving was a meritorious act, a good deed which brought about her forgiveness. It was not an act of grace but of good works. However, Kenneth Bailey points out that for over a thousand years this has been mistranslated. The word "for" in the statement should be translated "therefore."[8] "Her sins which are many are forgiven: **therefore** she loved much." **The Good News for Modern Man** version of the text supports this: "I tell you, then, the great love she has shown proves that her many sins have been forgiven."

But even of greater significance is that the parable Jesus tells supports this order: love resulting from forgiveness rather than love creating the possibility of forgiveness. Jesus says, "There were two men who owed money to a moneylender; one owed him five hundred dollars and the other fifty dollars. Neither one could pay him back, so he canceled the debts of both. Which one, then, will love him more?" Here quite obviously forgiveness comes before love.

Fuller catches this as he writes, "Her extravagant act of devotion is a sign that her sins, 'which were many,' have already been forgiven. How were they forgiven? By Jesus' acceptance of her, sinner though she was."[9] Therefore, forgiveness is an act of grace, and our love is a response to that act of God's gracious forgiveness.

Love and devotion to God are responses to the knowledge that he has forgiven us. This is extremely important in the realm of practical churchmanship. We so frequently exhort people that they should love God. What we should be doing is making forgiveness more of a reality in their lives. The message of God's unmerited, unearned gift of forgiveness creates the response of love that is so necessary if people are to enthusiastically labor and serve in his cause. Love is not something people are commanded to do, but it is the spontaneous expression of those who recognize and appreciate the gift of grace which is forgiveness. The announcement of forgiveness comes first, then the response of gratitude which results can be directed into channels of love and service.

A little boy was visiting his grandparents. And he was given his first sling-shot. He had great fun playing with it in the woods. He would take aim, let the stone fly, but he never hit a thing. Then on his way home for dinner, he cut through the backyard and saw grandmother's pet duck. He took aim and let the stone fly. It went straight to the mark and the duck fell dead. The little boy panicked. In frightened desperation he took the dead duck and hid it in the woodpile. Then he saw his sister Sally standing over by the corner of the house. She had seen the whole thing. They went into dinner. Sally said nothing. After dinner Grandmother said, "O.K., Sally, let's clear the table and wash the dishes." Sally said, "Oh, Grandmother, Johnny said he wanted to help you in the kitchen today. Didn't you, Johnny?" And then she whispered to him, "Remember the duck." So Johnny did the dishes. Later in the day Grandfather said, "It's a great day for fishing. What say, children, let's head for the river." But Grandmother said, "I'm sorry, Sally can't go. She promised to help me clean the house and get supper tonight." Sally smiled, "That's all been taken care of. Johnny said he wanted to help you today, didn't you, Johnny?" And she whispered, "Remember the duck!"

Now this went on for several days. Johnny did all the chores, his and those assigned to Sally. Finally he could stand it no longer, so he went to his grandmother and confessed all. His grandmother took him in her arms and said, "I know, Johnny. I was standing at the kitchen window and I saw the whole thing. I know you really didn't mean to do it. And because I love you I forgave you. The reason I haven't said anything to you is that I knew you knew I loved you and would forgive you. And I wondered just how long you would let Sally make a slave of you."

Isn't this our problem? We are forgiven people but so often we live as if we are not. We still operate as people enslaved by guilt, worrying over our wrongdoings and past sins, rather than rejoicing in the freedom God has given to us in Christ. What we need is not forgiveness. We have that in Christ. What we need is to fully realize that we are forgiven and then let this knowledge express itself in deeds of gratitude and love.

More Sin, More Love?

There is little doubt that Jesus used this parable not only to justify the actions of this woman and to attack Simon the fault-finder, but also to defend his association with sinners. Bruce comments that Jesus is saying in effect, "I repel not this woman, I accept gladly those demonstrations of devoted love, for I desire to be much loved."[10] Jesus associated with sinners and welcomed their attention because he knew that their expressions of love were sincere. They were not trying to get something from him; they were responding to the great thing he had done for them. As the parable states, they loved much because they had been forgiven much.

There is a danger here. People might conclude from this a need to commit greater sins so that they might experience greater forgiveness and therefore be able to show forth greater love. Now it is true that many who have succeeded in the art of sinning have become some of the most outstanding saints. Paul calls himself the "chief of sinners." The fact is that people with great energy,

28

powerful impulses, and strong emotions are capable of doing both extraordinary deeds of evil as well as goodness. Such people have the capacity and the faculty to hate or to love much. When this passionate energy for doing evil is converted to righteousness, the results are always unusual and outstanding. Saul, the fierce persecutor of Jesus, becomes Paul, the faithful proclaimer of Christ. However, to conclude from this that we should become persecutor before we can become proclaimer is an abuse of the meaning of this parable. The point is not just the greatness of the sin committed, but the extent of our realization of sin. It is the feeling of tremendous need, rather than the size of the sin that affects the appreciation of forgiveness.

All of us are sinners. Simon was a sinner within the Law in the same manner as the prostitute was outside the Law. What Simon needed was not to sin more, but to become aware of the sins that already marked his life. "He to whom much is forgiven" means, he who feels, recognizes, knows himself to be greatly in need of forgiveness. The point made by the parable is not the amount of sin, but the sense of it, which is measure of the gratitude to him who forgives it.[11]

A Broken Jar

A detail that is frequently overlooked is the broken alabaster jar of perfume. Wallace points out that this precious ointment was an essential tool of the prostitute's trade in the times of Jesus.[12] Prostitutes of the first century world would have a small flask of perfume hanging about their necks. Giving off a pleasant odor, it would attract customers. Now the breaking of this vital tool of her trade was a symbolic gesture indicating she had given up her old life and was adopting a new life style.

This action is also symbolic of the true meaning of

repentance in the New Testament. When we think of repentance today we associate it with being sorry for sins, or regret over wrongdoings. In the New Testament, however, repentance is a **change** or a **turning about.** When a caterpillar enters a cocoon and emerges as a butterfly this is called "metamorphosis." This comes from the same Greek word as does the word "repent." When Jesus begins his ministry with the message, "Repent for the Kingdom of God is at hand," he is not calling men to a life of remorse and sorrow; rather he is calling people to experience their lives being turned about and headed in a new direction. He is bringing in a new Kingdom and to live in that Kingdom people need to become new persons.

By the act of breaking the flask this woman is saying something very important about what the person of Jesus and his message of God's love and forgiveness meant to her life. The experience of forgiveness has turned her life about. She has been born again and is now ready and willing to begin a new life. And that is the true meaning of repentance. We are forgiven by grace and this experience makes of us new persons.

One of the outstanding preachers of the Lutheran Church tells the story that when he was a young boy living on a farm in the Midwest, his father told him that the spring rains were about to set in, and when they did the fields must be ready to receive them. The father told his son to go out into the north field and plow as much as he could before the rains began. So the young boy went into the field, but it wasn't long before some of his friends came strolling down the road with their fishing poles over their shoulders. They came over to the fence and leaning on the top rail called to him, "Come on, go fishing with us." The young boy responded that he was sorry, it was a great day for fishing but his father had given him definite instructions to plow the field.

His friends came back, "Ah, come, go with us. When we finish fishing, we'll all come back and help you. Together in an hour we can do what it would take all day for you to do by yourself." That sounded reasonable, so the young boy left the unfinished field and scampered down the road after his friends.

It was a great day for fishing and the hours passed lazily by. Suddenly the boy saw a drop of rain hit the surface of the pond, and then another. He looked up and saw the heavy dark clouds hovering overhead. Then he remembered the unplowed field. He dropped his fishing pole and headed for home as the rain came down. The faster he ran, the harder it began to rain, until, when he reached the farmhouse, the spring rains had set in with all their force. He walked up onto the back porch and opened the old screen door and stepped into the kitchen. There his father stood. He said nothing; he just reached down and unfastened the buckle of his belt. The little boy knew what was coming and he knew he deserved it. He headed toward the stairs, went up to his room, bent over his bed and waited for the punishment to begin. His father entered the room. Still the boy waited. The minutes passed and seemed like hours, and nothing happened. Then he looked slowly around and there kneeling by the door was his father, and he heard him pray, "Father in Heaven, creator of men, forgive my son for his neglect and make a responsible man of him."

The great theologian later confessed that the words of that prayer cut into his sensitive being more deeply than the sting of any whip. And then he added, "that night a boy died, but a **man was born.**"

This is the meaning of the parable of the Two Debtors. Unmerited forgiveness has the power to create new people. And we cannot listen to this parable without remembering that he who first told it went willingly to a place called Hill of the Skull. There they nailed his innocent hands to a cross erected by our many sins. There he hung with soldiers' mocking spit running down his face, because we rebel against our creator and are blind and deaf to his limitless love. With arms out-stretched on our cross he lifted his eyes upward and prayed, "Father forgive them; for they know not what they do." Noting so great a cost of our forgiveness, can we fail to recognize the extent of our sinfulness? We are the ones to whom much has been forgiven, therefore let us be much loving in all we do. The word of forgiveness echoes and re-echoes down the corridors of history breaking in again and again into the life of the church, and when it does, children die and adult persons of the faith are born.

Notes

1. Ronald S. Wallace, **Many Things in Parables,** (New York: Harper and Brothers, 1955), p. 95.
2. Archibald M. Hunter, **The Parables Then and Now,** (Philadelphia: Westminster, 1971), p. 53.
3. Kenneth E. Bailey, **New Perspectives on the Parables,** (Pittsburgh: Thesis Theological Cassettes, 1975).
4. Henry Ward Beecher, **The Original Plymouth Pulpit,** Vol. I, (Boston: Pilgrim Press, 1969), p. 211.
5. David M. Granskow, **Preaching of the Parables,** (Philadelphia: Fortress Press, 1972), p. 60.
6. Francis L. Filas, **The Parables of Jesus,** (New York Macmillan, 1959), p. 40.
7. Hillyer, Hawthorne Straton, **A Guide to the Parables of Jesus,** (Grand Rapids: Eerdmans, 1959), p. 119.
8. Kenneth E. Bailey, op. cit.
9. Reginald H. Fuller, **Preaching the New Lectionary: The Word of God for the Church Today,** (Collegeville, Minn.: Liturgical Press, 1974), p. 527.
10. Alexander Balmain Bruce, **The Parabolic Teachings of Christ,** (New York: George H. Doran), p. 250.
11. Marcus Dods, **The Parables of Our Lord,** (New York: Fleming H. Revell), p. 250.
12. Wallace, op. cit., p. 98.

A
First
Century
Mugging

2

THE PARABLE OF THE GOOD SAMARITAN
Luke 10:25-37

Several years ago there was an article in *Look* magazine entitled, "When You Get Mugged." It was written by the senior editor of *Look*, and he pointed out that our chances of getting mugged on the streets of the average city in the U.S.A. increase every year. Seven years later we know how right he was.

Since money is what most concerns the mugger, the advice given by Ira Mothner in his article was, "When you get mugged, give up, shut up, and pay up."

Our parable of the Good Samaritan is a story about a first century mugging. Apparently the merchant in our story, when he was attacked by robbers, did not "give up, shut up, and pay up," but resisted and fought back to protect his property. So the robbers beat him up, leaving him half dead in the ditch by the side of the road. It happened on the long steep descent through the mountains on the road from Jerusalem down to Jericho. It was a notorious haunt of robbers and seldom did anyone travel this way alone. To do so was to invite disaster. Therefore, the fact that the man was robbed on this road was not unusual. What was unusual and surprising about the story is that the hero was a Samaritan.

The Samaritans Then And Now

Our parable is the story of a good Samaritan. Hospitals, churches and institutions of mercy the world over have been named in his honor. But history has not been good to his people. Once numbering in the tens of thousands, there are today only a few hundred

Samaritans still surviving in a wretched corner of their once great city, now an Arab town called Nablus, just over the Israeli border in Jordan. They are poverty-stricken and have no home to call their own. They live in borrowed tents from their good neighbors, the Arabs of Jordan.

To really understand how the Jews in Jesus' day felt about the Samaritans, one need only to pick up the daily newspaper and see the hate and the suspicion that now exists between Jew and Arab in the Near East. As the Jews now hate and despise their neighbors the Arabs, so they once reacted toward the Samaritans.

The rift between the Samaritans and the main body of Judaism began in the fifth century B.C. when Ezra led the tribes of Israel back to Jerusalem from their captivity in Babylon. The Jews who lived in and near Samaria had escaped the long period of exile. They remained and lived with their conquerors and intermarried with them. Because of this Ezra looked upon them as unclean. When the Samaritans offered to help rebuild the temple at Jerusalem, Ezra refused them. The Samaritans were outraged and built a rival temple on Mount Gerizim. A long and bitter conflict followed. By the time of Jesus the spite fence between Jew and Samaritan was strongly established. They hated each other, as Jew and Arab hate each other today. In our text the Jewish lawyer could not bring himself to mention the name "Samaritan," so in answer to Jesus' question at he end of the parable, he said, "The **one** who was kind to him."

Therefore, the fact that Jesus told a story where a Samaritan was the hero is almost unbelievable. It must have so shocked the original Jewish listener that it is a wonder the story was ever remembered and recorded.

Today, however, "good" and "Samaritan" are almost synonymous in the minds of the average listening congregation. The Samaritans, as we pointed out above, are almost an extinct people and the only Samaritan we know about is the man in the story Jesus told. However, if the parable is to be fully understood, the social and religious explosive connotations of the word "Samaritan" need to be kept in mind. Jesus is telling the story about a hated enemy of his people who was in a certain situation, and in his response, superior to the Jewish characters of the story. It would be as if Jesus were to tell to the Jews in Jerusalem today a story about a good Arab.

A Tricky Lawyer

Luke begins the account by noting that a lawyer came to Jesus and addressed him as "Rabbi," which means "teacher" or "master." This indicates that the lawyer recognized Jesus as of equal status. The lawyer was a natural born debater. He was a man who delighted in discussing and arguing religious issues. He was intelligent, well-informed, skilled in clever logic, and a man of sound reasoning.

Luke makes it clear that he came to test Jesus. He wanted to see just how well-informed this young teacher from Nazareth was. So the lawyer initiates the debate with a question, "What must I do to inherit eternal life?" (Note the discussion of this question at the end of the chapter.) The question was purely academic. This lawyer was a mental athlete. He liked to exercise the muscles of his mind and publicly display the biceps of his cleverness.

Our Lord, however, was his match. He answered the question with a well-tested technique. He asked another question, "What is written in the Law?" The lawyer was delighted with this question. He knew the answer and rattled forth the Law — to the letter: "You shall love the Lord your God with all your heart, and with all your mind; and, you must love your neighbor as yourself."

The next move belonged to Jesus and he delivers a

telling blow. He says, "Your answer is correct, do this and you will live." This brought the theoretical discussion to a temporary standstill. Our Lord had brought the issue down to the practical level and it was obvious at once that the lawyer's problem came not with a distant God but with a present neighbor. The lawyer got the point and he felt it deeply for he knew that he did not love his neighbors.

But the lawyer is a clever man and he will not take such a blow lying down. He will not let the conversation end on such a practical level. So he says, "And who is my neighbor?" You see immediately how he brings the discussion back to the theoretical level where he feels comfortable. He avoids the obvious implications of our Lord to get out and do something about his beliefs, by asking another abstract question.

How often we encounter this same tactical maneuver when trying to get a child to go to bed. The directive is clear and simple, "It's time to go to bed." But the child will think about a hundred and one things that he must talk about. He will bring up question after question to hold off the inevitable and postpone the demanded action.

And as adults we are no different. We know that discussion is an excellent method of avoiding action. But we are more sophisticated in our responses. When faced with stewardship, evangelism, or the expansion of the church facilities, we form a committee to discuss the matter. We thereby substitute talk for action. Someone has said that there is little doubt that if St. Peter had appointed a committee to plan for Pentecost, it would never have come off. So the lawyer stands before us as an excellent example that discussion is the best means to avoid action.

Brunner at this point comments that it is here in this issue of knowing and doing that the New Testament adds something to the Old Testament. Brunner asks what is added: "Everything is added and nothing is added."[1] Both testaments center on the love for God and neighbor. But what is just taught and promised in the Old Testament is fulfilled in the New. What is emphasized in the New Testament is the living out of the will of God. Brunner writes, "If a composer has put down on paper a new symphony — the parts are written out to the last note — what then may be added? Nothing and everything. The notes must become sounds, the symphony must be played."[2] So Jesus says to the lawyer, "You have the right symphony, now play it." And as he presents this directive to "do this," he is presenting the uniqueness of the New Testament where he as the Son of Man does the will of God and empowers us to do the same.

The Law Of Love

Eta Linnemann believes that the lawyer asked for a definition of "neighbor" because definitions, like laws, give a certainty and a security behind which we can hide and avoid the necessity of a daily encounter with God. She writes, "For to know what can be required of me is like a shell inside which one can live peacefully because everything inside it is familiar."[3] Both law and definition give us power over a situation. They place in our hands a perfectly laid out plan of action which we can use to control the situation. With such a plan we really don't need God, because we do not have to continually struggle to know his will. We have it in our pocket.

A certain man was travelling from one large city to another and he saw a traveler being attacked by bandits in the road ahead. "What must I do?" he asked himself. Being a Christian he immediately reached into his pocket and pulled out a copy of the New Testament. He turned quickly to the index and looked up the word "robbery." It referred him to the Gospel according to St. Luke, chapter ten, verses twenty-three to thirty-seven.

There he read the parable of the Good Samaritan. But not understanding exactly what it meant, he reached in his other pocket and took out a layman's commentary on the book of Luke. There he found that the parable presented the "Law of Love," which was defined as having compassion, binding up and treating the wounds of an injured neighbor.

Satisfied that he had found the right rule, the man hid behind some rocks and watched as the bandits finished beating up the poor traveler and finally threw him in the ditch by the side of the road. Now the man thought it was time for Christian service, so when he was sure that the bandits were a safe distance away, our hero ventured out to help his neighbor. He did exactly what the parable and its "Law of Love" instructed him to do. He bound up the wounds, poured oil and a little wine on them and then took him to the nearest motel and paid for his lodging.

The man left the motel proud and satisfied with himself. He had been a good Christian Samaritan. He had fulfilled the "Law of Love" to the letter and God would certainly reward him someday for being such a good neighbor.

Now it is obvious that anyone who hides behind the rocks while his neighbor is nearly being beaten to death is hardly a good neighbor. Making a rule out of the "Law of Love" limited his service and blinded him to what God's will was for him in that particular situation. He thought that he didn't have to struggle to find God's will. It was defined in his little books of rules and regulations.

Brunner writes, "It is the curse of a certain knowlege-ability of the Scriptures to take the Bible as a pretext for the purpose of bypassing God."[4] And that is exactly what we do when we make a law out of love and hide behind definitions of "neighbor" to avoid being a good neighbor to everyone.

The Jews had always regarded the term "neighbor" as

a very limited concept. When they read in Lev. 19:18, "You shall love your neighbor as yourself," they interpreted it to mean love your fellow Jews. The commandment did not include Gentiles or heretical Samaritans. In the light of this, we can see that the lawyer wanted to know who his neighbor was so he could know with certainty to whom he did not have to be a good neighbor.

Christ, however, will not fall into this trap. Instead of giving an answer or a definition, he tells a story. The story is about a situation in which a Samaritan acted in direct response to **that** situation. He encountered the will of God not in a prescribed commandment of the law but in the need of a beaten and robbed person.

The lawyer was a typical example of the people Christ was constantly coming up against — good people who knew the Law of God and who equated it with the will of God. Their theology was: know the Law and that is all you need. Jesus came to bring something greater than the Law. That is why he chose a Samaritan as the hero of his story, because his fellow Jews believed that a Samaritan would know nothing of the true Law of God. And the stinging point of his story is that a man who did not know the Law nevertheless fulfilled the **will** of God. He fulfilled the will of God because he was alert and sensitive to what God required of him in a particular situation. He was directed to act by the requirement of need in the situation he faced. A fellow human was in need and he met it. Christ says that this is fulfilling the will of God.

A Damning Indictment

One of the most controversial issues concerning the parable is whether or not the parable of the Good Samaritan really answers the question the lawyer asked. Hunter[5] says that it does not. Rather it shows the lawyer that he has asked the wrong question. The right question is not **who** is my neighbor, but to **whom** can I be a good neighbor? And to this question the parable answers, "Anyone whose need serves a claim on my help."[6]

Then Hunter adds that the parable is not just about a man who did a good deed; rather it is a "damning indictment"[7] of all racial and religious superiority.

A Slap In The Face

Granskou also holds that the parable does not answer the question, "Who is my neighbor?" Rather it is an "offensive statement,"[8] a slap in the face to the people of God, that they should come up to the level of virtue found in the outside world. The parable does not instruct me as to the identity of my neighbor, "but asks me to contemplate the unpleasant fact that those who are outside my circle and religion might be better persons than I."

This parable is not directed to the Jews alone, but against all smugness. The purpose of the parable, according to Granskou, is not just to tell us to go out and help those in need, but to realize that mercy is often shown in the world by men and women who are not Christians. The people in the world may be more "Christ-like" in their actions than we are.

No Questions Asked

C.W.F. Smith, speaking to the interpretation that anyone in need is to be considered "neighbor," states that this would be a justifiable exegesis if the story were designed to answer the lawyer's question, which it is not. "As a matter of fact," Smith says, "this is precisely **not** the point"[9] of the parable.

The parable begins with the phrase, "A man." No details are given about him. He is anonymous because he is not the central actor. He is the object, not the subject, of the story. Attention is directed away from him to the Samaritan, the priest and the Levite. The Samaritan is the surprise element of the story. He stands in contrast over against the priest and the Levite. In the story his role is to show what the priest and the Levite should have done but did not. Therefore, Smith takes the position that Jesus used the parable to attack the Jewish hierarchy.[10] This group failed to do the will of God, but the hated heretic did it.

Jesus saw the will of God for Israel to be the role of servants of God, and therefore to be neighbors to all with no questions asked. The members of the hierarchy of Israel, on the other hand, saw themselves as "princes" to be served and honored. So Jesus directed the parable of the Good Samaritan as an attack against the mistaken attitude of the Jewish hierarchy toward the people outside the Jewish race, and at the same time against the mistaken attitude the hierarchy had toward itself and its role in human history.

Victim Of Blood Road

In contrast to those who believe the parable does **not** answer the question of the lawyer, Wallace emphatically believes that it does. In fact, Wallace states that the answer to the question "shines out so clearly that not even the lawyer could argue against the meaning which Jesus intended."[11]

According to Wallace the parable defines "neighbor" as all the victims of the "Blood Road," which is the road of life, the road of the world that is strewn with the helpless casualties of daily life.[12] Jesus is directing the attention of the lawyer away from the sheltered world of contemplation and theological speculation to the real world where people struggle with hatred, greed and crime. And at the same time he pictures our indifference to what is happening on the "Blood Road."

Wallace adds that Jesus is also giving a picture of himself in this parable. He came to the "Blood Road" to heal and comfort, and raise up fallen people to health and freedom. And our Lord says to us in this parable, "I have been a neighbor to you. I have shown you what love is like. Go and do thou likewise."

Who Is My God?

Glen aligns himself with those who believe the parable answers the question of the lawyer. He comments, "Who is my neighbor is answered by the recognition that if one acts like a neighbor, one will discover who his neighbor is."[13]

This unique thing Glen has to say concerning this parable is that he finds within it not only the answer to the question, "Who is my neighbor?" but he finds here also the answer to the question, "Who is my God?"[14] For the God of the Bible identifies himself with all the victims of injustice and suffering. When we pass by the man on the other side, this is "tantamount to passing the God of the Bible by on the other side."[15]

Glen also believes that we can see ourselves in the role of the victim. He reveals our situations of misfortune and injustice. In such a state God comes to us and helps us with "strange Samaritan hands."[16]

The conclusion Glen comes to is very suggestive for a sermonic approach to the parable. He says that every figure in the parable reveals to us "ourselves in relation to others and to the God of grace to whom we belong."[17] The victim reveals our need for God. The Samaritan reveals "the neighborliness by means of which through us God would reveal his love to the broken and bruised, the hopeless and abandoned, along the road of life."[18]

Sensitivity

Eta Linnemann believes the difficulty of determining

whether or not Jesus answers the lawyer's question arises because "we ascribe a mistaken function to verse 36. We assume that here the question of verse 29 is to be resumed, so as to get a definite answer. But the story itself, nothing else, is the answer to the question."[19] The meaning of the story is that a fellow human being was in need and therefore he is a neighbor.

Linnemann adds that the parable is not simply a demand to go and do as the Samaritan did. Rather it is Jesus calling us from a view of the "world simply as one that is basically controlled by law that is as complete as possible, and on to the movement of authentic living."[20]

What this means is that what God desires for our lives is not to be found in the law but is revealed in the situations of life which confront us. We are not to follow step by step what the Samaritan did, but we are to be motivated to action in the same decisive way the Samaritan was motivated to act. We are to let ourselves be governed completely by the confrontation of need. This means that it is not just this or that specific act that we must do, but our whole attitude toward life that needs to be altered. What is needed is not a law but a keen sensitivity to the claims and the demands life makes upon us.

This makes a great deal of sense when seen in the light of Paul's teaching that we as Christians are to be governed not by the Law but by the Holy Spirit. The contrast then becomes the contrast between Mount Sinai and the Garden of Gethsemane. An ethical life directed from Mount Sinai would be a life governed by a code of written rules. But a life directed from Gethsemane would be a continual prayer-like struggle with the living God searching for his guiding will. Each time we are faced with a question or a decision we depend not on a law to govern our actions but the Holy Spirit of God to empower and direct our actions.

In practice such ethical living would demand that the

person be continually involved with Holy Scripture for it is the Word of God that keeps us sensitive and aware of the directives of the Holy Spirit. Johnny Valentine, by reputation the most notorious safe-cracker in the history of crime, would take sandpaper and sand the ends of his fingers until the nerve ends were raw, thereby making his fingers hypersensitive and enabling him to feel the delicate movement of the pistons that made up the lock of the safe. He could actually feel the pistons drop into place as he turned the dial. So the Holy Scriptures sand away the protective covering of our senses so that the nerve ends of our feelings and thoughts become keen and sharp to every direction of guidance the Holy Spirit might offer us.

In the light of Linnemann's interpretation of this parable, God calls us through the parable of the Good Samaritan to be adventurous and creative in our righteousness. God does not want us to be like the lawyer, arguing and debating over the definition of "neighbor." Rather God wants us to be like the Samaritan — out on the road of life responding freely and creatively under the direction of the Holy Spirit to every human need that might confront us.

Conflict Of Obligations

Harvey sees in the reaction of the priest and the Levite not an expression of a lack of love, but a "conflict of obligations."[21] The man was near death and if he died in their arms this would inflict ritual defilement and they would not be able to fulfill their duties and obligations to God. It was, therefore, a case of the obligations of loyalty overcoming love, caution overcoming charity, religious duty overcoming human decency, ritual overcoming righteousness.

The parable was not designed to teach love of neighbor. According to Harvey this was so completely accepted by the Jews that it needed no parable. Rather it is a parable designed to shock the Jews out of their limited idea of who their neighbor was. Everyone — anyone, particularly those who are different, is to be seen as a neighbor. The parable, Harvey concludes, is directed against the "exclusive nationalism of the Jewish people in the time of Jesus; but there has never yet been a society or a civilization in which it would have no relevance."[22] To those who would wave flags and declare that "charity begins at home," this parable stands as a defiant warning.

Beyond The Inn

The Good Samaritan is frequently held up as an example par excellence of the Christian virtue of service to our neighbor. However, when we look at the parable itself, there is no such exaggerated claim. Christ is simply describing how any person should react to someone who is in need. It is a definition of being a neighbor but not a definition of what it means to be a Christian. The terms are related, but they are not synonymous.

In the light of the total revelation of the New Testament, the action of the Good Samaritan is at best only "first aid." The Good Samaritan offered help, bound up his wounds and took him to the inn, but he did not heal the needy man. The Christian concept of service demands much more. It demands not **first aid** but **cross aid,** which means that in our service to those in need we must go beyond the inn, where people are only helped, to the cross where they are healed.

The parable of the Good Samaritan presents us with an excellent example of what is expected of us as good neighbors, but it does not present the extent to which we should go as Christians. The truth is, Christian service only begins at the inn. This does not mean that we use our service in the world as a gimmick to bring people to

Jesus Christ, but that all of our efforts of service should be in the name of Jesus Christ and a means by which people might come to know the love of Christ.

As humans we love and offer service to those in need, but our concern as Christians must not stop here. We realize that people need more than physical and material help. They need to find meaning and purpose for their lives. It is a worthwhile service to stand a fallen person on his feet, but it is a fruitless service unless that person is given a desire to walk, a reason to walk, and a place to walk to.

Beyond the inn is the cross. Here people are not only helped and healed, but are also given dignity and purpose and meaning for their lives. Here they discover that they have value because they are loved. Here they are freed from their past mistakes and given a new option for living. Here plateaus of boredom are broken, loneliness finds companionship, and tragedies are turned into moments of victory and joy. This is the **cross aid** that people so desperately need, and should be the purpose of all Christian service in the world.

It should also be noted that there is an ultimate aspect to true Christian service. It is not a temporary good deed done, but a basic change in the very pattern of life. Christ went to the cross not just to help and heal those who fall victim to robbers on the road of life, but he placed himself in the center of that road to take unto himself all the future killing blows aimed at the underpriviledged and the oppressed. In this Christ proved himself to be the great neighbor to all mankind. He went to the cross so that we could not be just **patched up** but **lifted up** to a new life. He went to the cross so that all the threatening roads of danger and death might be made safe. He went to the cross and died so that we might be free to live together as brothers and sisters, and that all the roads of life might be safe and free.

The Good Victim

Most scholars assume that the man in the ditch was a Jew. If this were true then the ordinary common people who first heard this parable must have seen in the victim in the ditch a symbolic picture of their own sorry condition. As the chosen people of God they had traveled the road of robbers. They had been cast down by foreign oppressors and beaten up by their own leaders. When they heard that the priest and the Levite passed by on the other side and did nothing for the injured man, they must have thought in their own minds, "How true!"

Next they expected that the story would mention a Jewish layman who came along and helped the poor man in the ditch. This would have made for a great story and would have pleased the crowd no end. But they are surprised because Jesus doesn't say a layman, he says a Samaritan. That stung the ears of the listeners and really upset them.

Yet this is the real crux and climax of the story. Help comes from an unexpected source. And to heighten the shock, an **unwanted** source — the hated Samaritan. The basic question now becomes not, "Who is my neighbor?" but "Are you willing to accept help from a hated enemy?" Is the man in the ditch in such desperate need and so aware of his total helplessness that he will accept help from anyone — even a Samaritan? In the story the Jew does accept the help of a Samaritan.

The Jews were quick to see themselves beside the man in the ditch and the point Christ was making struck home. If you are desperate enough to accept help from a Samaritan then you might just be in a proper state of mind to turn to a carpenter's son from Nazareth and see him as your ultimate help. Christ may not look like much to the Jews. but he is all they have.

The parable of the Good Samaritan is such a fascinating story that we tend to overlook the decisive point of who it was that told this story. And we forget the fact that because Jesus told this story and many others like it, he was branded a traitor, condemned as a blasphemer of God, and eventually crucified as a heretic. Christ used his parables as weapons of attack. They were swords of sharp truth intended to cut through the very heart of the basic issues that faced the average man in the street.

In our pious propriety we easily read our own ideas into the parable and treat this parable of the Good Samaritan as a harmless little moral fable teaching that we should all be good little Samaritans and help our neighbors. But Jesus would never have gotten into trouble and marched up Calvary to a cross for telling harmless little moral ditties. When we are satisfied to milk a moral nugget from the parable, we overlook the situation of conflict for which the parable was intended. For example, when we make of the parable of the Good Samaritan a moral fable of neighborliness, we miss the stinging attack it contains against the misguided leadership of the Jewish people who were preoccupied with rules and regulations and had no concern for the needs of the common people. At the same time we miss the loving appeal of God within this parable that is directed to the people in the ditch of life, desperate and desolate. And most tragic of all, we fail to hear the call to surrender and accept help — the help that has come from God in Christ.

As the Samaritan was a surprising and shocking hero in the story, so Christ was a shocking and surprising savior in the current life situation of the Jews. Jesus was not the hero they expected would come to meet their needs. They wanted a warrior-like Davidic Messiah. A carpenter's son who spoke of peace hardly measured up to their expectations. So, you see, this is not just a story about a Good Samaritan that helped a man in need; it is at the same time a story of a victim that was **good** because he was willing to accept help from a Samaritan.

It is sometimes difficult to help a man in need, but it is equally difficult to **accept** help, especially when that acceptance involves our humiliation. Did you ever stumble and fall in a public place? You appreciated attempts to help you up, but you would rather have been unnoticed and gotten up by yourself. Well, the parable of the Good Samaritan was directed to the common Jew seeking to find out if he was aware enough of his help- lessness to overcome his prejudices and expectations of a savior to see in Jesus the mark of Messiahship.

Jesus came to his people. At first they misunderstood him. And when they finally began to understand him, they rejected him. He was not the Messiah they expected and wanted. Because the Jews were a hard-hearted people, God realized that what they needed was not a teacher with a neat little bag of moral and ethical truths. No, they needed a suffering servant savior who would be willing to climb down into the ditch where men had fallen and with a cross lift them up to a new life, in a Kingdom newly come. The parable asks the question, "Are you willing to accept this help when it comes?"

Now, like the Jews to whom this story was originally told, we are people in a ditch. I am not sure of the exact dimensions or depths of your particular ditch, or how or why you got there. It may be that in the past you did something terribly wrong and are in a ditch of guilt. It may be that you failed to get out of life what you really wanted, and are in a ditch of disappointment and despair. It may be nothing has any meaning or purpose for you and you are in a ditch of meaninglessness. It may be that you are just plain bored with it all. But whatever the dimension or description or definition you choose, we are all in one way or another ditch dwellers. And the tragedy is that we so often desperately try to save ourselves trying to avoid the embarrassment of admit- ting our helplessness. Sometimes we think the answer is a ladder that will enable us to climb out — a ladder such as technology, science, education, social action. Some of us think the answer is moral fortitude — becoming so good that we will sprout wings and fly out like haloed angels. Many in our generation have just given up and have accepted the destiny of ditch dwelling and applied first aid to our wounds with drugs and drink. But whether we fight or accept with resignation, or get drunk to forget about it, one thing is sure, eventually we will come to the realization the ditch is just too deep, and we must get help from outside ourselves.

And this needs to be added: this ditch in which we are all condemned to dwell has a final depth of darkness called "death," which will ultimately defeat all our efforts. No amount of education, culture, or cleverness can deliver us from this final defeat of self-dependence. If help is to come it must come from above and beyond ourselves.

And this is the gospel. Christ comes to us as the hated Samaritan came to the helpless man in our parable. Christ comes to us with help and healing. Christ comes freely and without invitation. He comes when we do not call out to him. He comes even when we do not want him. And the only issue for us as for the Jew in the ditch is — are we willing to accept the help when it comes?

It isn't easy to admit that we are wrong. It isn't easy to admit that we need help and cannot help ourselves. It pierces our pride and shatters to pieces our self-dependence. It isn't easy to give up and accept help from such an unexpected, illogical, unreasonable source as a Jewish carpenter's son from the first century who came to reveal a strange and totally gracious God who asks nothing from us except our nothingness.

There is a popular book entitled *I'm O.K., You're O.K.* Now this may be an attractive psychology, but it is rotten theology. For the Gospel declares, "You're not O.K. and I'm not O.K. but that's O.K. with God." God accepts us as we are, where we are, and the deeper the ditch the greater God's reach of grace. Our only response is to surrender to that grip of grace, accept our acceptance, and we are born anew into the Kingdom of God.

God's first step down to us is our first step up to him. Lincoln said, "A man never stands so tall as when he is on his knees before God." So it has been the testimony of every saint that has ever walked across the pages of human history — God's grace undeservedly given to the lowly. St. Francis of Assisi said as he was dying, "Place me on the floor. I want to die where I found life — at the feet of my Lord." This is the gospel — the surprising, unexpected news that God comes to us where we are, as we are, ditch dwellers, and by his good grace and gracious goodness raises us up, heals us and gives us a new and abundant life. The Lord is my Good Samaritan — I shall not want.

Being Truly Human

We have considered the effect the conflict between Jew and Samaritan had on the interpretation of this parable. We are also familiar with the fierce hatred and prejudice that existed between Jew and Gentile in the days of our Lord. But we frequently overlook the violent hatred among the various political-religious groups within Judaism itself in addition to the Samaritan Jewish conflict.

Four major groups within Judaism were constantly at each other's throats — the Pharisees, the Sadducees, the Zealots, and the Essenes. Our acquaintance with the Pharisees and the Sadducees is well established by the frequency of our encounter with these two groups as they attack our Lord and his teachings in the gospel accounts. We also know something about the Zealots because of Judas. We know that the Zealots were a militant group constantly inciting the people to active rebellion against the Roman oppressors.

The Essenes are perhaps lesser known. They were the proteges of Herod the Great and considered to be collaborators with the occupying Roman power. The Essenes lived a monastic kind of life, refusing to observe some of the essential Jewish practices and were bitterly opposed to the religious "Establishment" of the Pharisees and Sadducees. Because of this and for several other reasons there was a special kind of malice that existed between the Zealots and the Essenes — a hatred that was cherished as a sacred duty.

Edmund Flood in his book *Parables of Jesus* finds in this conflict between the Zealots and the Essenes some interesting and provocative insights into the meaning of the parable of the Good Samaritan.

Remembering the Essenes had several established strong monastic communities near Jericho, Flood presents the story of the Good Samaritan as an account of a Zealot attacking an Essene traveler.

Defending this interpretation, Flood points out that an ordinary robber would simply have taken the victim's valuables, but the details of the story point up the fact that the robber takes off the victim's garments and then beats him up. The Essenes were often identified by the expensive and elegant clothes of white linen which they wore. To a Zealot, these garments would be symbolic of the Essenes' cooperation with Herod and the Romans. In addition, white linen garments were considered the exclusive dress of the priests. Therefore, the very attire of the Essene traveler would have irritated the Zealot and provoked him to tear the fine fabric from the body of his hated political opponent.

Flood further points out that what we have here in the story of the Good Samaritan is not the account of a robbery at all. Flood comments:

The other unusual feature of this robbery was that it was not done in order to rob at all. This would have been clear to the original audience because they knew that "robber" was the cryptic name for a Zealot. The motive was not to rob because anyway Essenes were not allowed to carry money. It was to express indignation, not to rob, that the man was so badly wounded.[23]

When the Sadducess passed by the man in the ditch, they too regarded him as their enemy. They more than likely thought in their minds, "So what if this man is dying. One less Essene is no serious loss." The priest and the levite passed by with similar disdain, according to Flood. So the poor injured man was ignored by his own people because he represented an undesireable dissenter within their own race.

Then came the Samaritan. He had reasons for hating the pitiful victim by the side of the road as had the Zealot, the Sadducees and the priest, but he stopped. Forgetting the five centuries of prejudice and hatred, he regarded the fallen traveler simply as a man, and he helped him.

Now what does this interpretation of Flood say to us today? It suggests that the word "neighbor" needs not only to be **expanded** to include people of different races and nationalties from our own, but the word "neighbor" needs to be **contracted** to include those close to us.

As we have pointed out above in our discussion, many interpreters of this parable stress the fact that the Jews had normally taken the word "neighbor" and narrowed its meaning to include only their own countrymen. Therefore, we should not make the same mistake. Jesus is telling us here to broaden and expand our concept of "Who is my neighbor?" This is a valid point; but it is equally true that often we need to narrow the word "neighbor" even more than we do to include persons who live next door, particularly when they are people we dislike for one reason or another.

There is a common saying, "With friends like this who needs enemies?" This certainly could have been the response of the victim as he lay in the ditch injured and watched his fellow countrymen pass him by. But then many times the people most difficult to help and treat as neighbors are those closest to us.

During the struggle between the blacks and the whites in our country, it was often the blacks who suffered most from the hands of other blacks. When the black militants rioted in the streets burning and looting, it was often the black store owners who endured the greatest property damage. Many of my black friends told me that during these difficult times of social change, they lived in terror behind bolted doors, fearing the harm their own radical black brothers might do to them.

Statistics bear out the fact that most people are murdered not by strangers but by people they know. In many cases both the murdered victim and the vicious killer are members of the same family.

Therefore, in our consideration of the possible interpretations of the parable of the Good Samaritan, we must not overlook the fact that this ill-fated fellow of the Jericho road was a victim of his own people. It was an atrocity of Jew against Jew. This means for us that the "enemy" we are to love is not always one of a different color, ethnic background, or of a country other than our own. He is often our next door neighbor, fellow church member, or even our own family. The point of the parable of the Good Samaritan is that we are to help those we have good reasons to hate. It is to love the unlovely and unlovable. It is to serve those we don't like. It is to help those we hate.

This interpretation of the parable is not easy to hear; but then the directives of Jesus are never easy. In most cases our Lord calls us to do exactly what we don't want to do. His words come to us frequently to convict, to collide with our commonly held ideas and opinions, to sting us at the point of our most sensitive vulnerability.

This is so not because God delights in placing upon us

injurious obligations; but he hurts us in order to heal us. What Jesus says is for real! We by our very natures possess habits of mind, and patterns of action that prevent us from being the full human personalities God intends us to be. It is for our own growth and development that God hits us where it hurts.

Our Lord is never satisified with neat little moral teachings such as, "Do unto others as you would have them do unto you." Rather Jesus presents to us life as it is to be lived in the Kingdom of God which he ushers in. He presents to us the theological insight that **when we do unto others we become what we do.** Prejudice, hatred, jealousy, and greed are self-destructive! In our inhuman treatment of others we destroy our own humanity.

The Good Samaritan was **good** not simply because he did a good deed and won for himself one more merit before God, or one more "star in his heavenly crown." No! The Samaritan was called good because he reacted to another person as a **person** and not as a member of a pre-established category — a Zealot, Pharisee, Sadducee, or Essene. By his humane act, he became himself a true and real human being. He became the person God intended him to be. The parable of the Good Samaritan perhaps would be better entitled **The Parable of the Good Person,** or **The Parable of Being Truly Human.**

Spark Starters

There is so much more that should be said about the preaching values of the parable of the Good Samaritan but space is limited. We have only been able in this chapter to touch the highlights of the main interpretations. However, there are a few stimulating ideas that might be mentioned briefly in the hopes that they will spark the imagination to fuller developments in a sermon:

1. Mercy is related to misery. The Good Samaritan did not lecture or preach to the man in the ditch concerning his foolish practice of traveling a dangerous road unprotected. This is no time to attempt to convert that man; it is only the time for comforting him.

2. Your neighbor may be the man you hate as the parable suggested was true for the Samaritan. However, as you help the one you hate, you can learn to love him. We do not begin service by loving our neighbor. We begin by helping him. As we help him we can come to love him.

3. There are three basic attitudes expressed in the parable. First the robber's attitude was, "Beat them up." The priest and the Levite's attitude was, "Pass them up." The Samaritan's attitude was, "Pick them up."

4. Many people attempt to see God by looking up. The parable suggests you find God by looking down — down into the ditch of broken lives where men cry out in need.

5. Our Lord wanted to show the lawyer that the moral problems he has are due to the religious problem he is. An unloving man is always his own worst enemy. He needs help not to find, but to become the right kind of neighbor.

6. Most people when they consider serving people in need think in terms of reaching down and pulling people up. This makes service a condescending action. We take care of their needs, but we rob them of their dignity. So often we injure people as we are attempting to heal them. In the parable the Good Samaritan gets down from his beast and places the injured man on it. He gets down where the man is — in the ditch — and that gives a whole new perspective to service. If we really put ourselves into the shoes of the person in need, more of us would find it is easier to lift up than to pull up.[24]

7. This little parable teaches us the three "littles" of genuine love: (a) the little that love needs to know — is he our kind, rich or poor, orthodox or heterodox? — no matter, (b) the little that love needs to ask — anyone who

has gone through the anguish of the barrage of questions that have to be answered at a hospital's emergency door appreciates the first aid this man gives, and (c) the little that love needs to have in the way of resources. He had no first aid kit. He made do with a homemade tourniquet ripped from his own robe. He had no antibiotics but used his own oil and wine instead.[25]

8. The little phrase, "By chance," is provocative. Jesus says, "Now by chance a priest was going down the road . . ." Here was a chance for the priest to show what his faith in Jehovah really meant. Here was the chance of a lifetime for the Levite to justify his whole reason for living. Sometimes the most heroic opportunities in life are thrust upon us by chance.[26]

Postscript
The Question Of Eternal Life

It is interesting to note that few if any interpreters deal with the first question of the lawyer, "What must I do to inherit eternal life?" For the person in the pew this is equally as important as the question, "Who is my neighbor?", if not more so. Now it may be that the question is apparently answered by Jesus that we will inherit eternal life if we know the law of God and do it. Therefore, the question needs no more consideration. However, to understand the answer does not necessarily mean that we understand the question. What did the lawyer in the text mean when he asked about eternal life? A great deal depends on how you interpret the term "eternal life." This phrase has various meanings and connotations in the Bible. It does not simply mean "heaven" as we commonly use that word.

The word used here is **aionios** which literally means "belonging to the age." It is not so much a quantity of life — a long life — as it is a quality of life — the good life. The lawyer being a Jew would not be concerned so much with immortality in the next world as with the morality of this world. His concern would be how he could live a life in fellowship with God. What the lawyer is really asking is not, "How will I get to heaven when I die?", which is what most listeners think when they hear the question, "What must I do to inherit eternal life?" Rather what he is asking is, "How can I know the good life, the full life, the abundant life?" He is asking how he can live right now in a right relationship with his God.

Now it should also be added that whenever the term "eternal life" is used in the New Testament, it in most cases refers to a life which is a free gift of God in Christ.

When the parable of the Good Samaritan is seen in the light of the statements above, some interesting insights emerge. Service to our fellowman and becoming a good neighbor are not something that we do to receive some future blessing; rather, they are what we do now because we have already received a blessing. In the story of the Good Samaritan Jesus is not telling the lawyer and us how we **should** act, but how we **will** act when we stand in a right relationship to God. When we surrender ourselves to Christ we are in the right relationship to God, and we are made good neighbors.

Brunner catches this when he writes concerning the parable, "Neighborly love is life from God himself. This is the central affirmation of the biblical message. It comes by the Holy Spirit. God is patient and does not give up until he wins power over us through his word and makes of us loving people. Through Jesus Christ he breaks the spell of evil in us and opens us up to the way of love."[26]

The parable of the Good Samaritan, therefore, is not law but gospel. It is not a moral admonition that we should love our neighbors, but it is a spiritual insight into what divine grace does to a person when it enters into his life. Grace makes of each of us a lover of all people, a servant to all in need, and a good neighbor to the world.

The lawyer asks Jesus, "What must I do to get the good life?" Jesus answers, "The good life is a gift from God, and when you get it you will be like the Samaritan who helped even his hated enemy, the Jew."

Notes

1. Emil Brunner, **Sowing and Reaping,** (Richmond, Va.: John Knox Press, 1946), p. 52.
2. Ibid., p. 52.
3. Eta Linnemann, **Jesus of the Parables,** (New York: Harper and Row, 1946), p. 52
4. Brunner, op. cit., p. 54.
5. Archibald M. Hunter, **The Parables Then and Now,** (Philadelphia: Westminster, 1971), p. 109.
6. Ibid., p. 110.
7. Ibid., p. 111.
8. David M. Granskou, **Preaching on the Parables,** (Philadelphia: Fortress Press, 1972), p. 81.
9. Charles W. F. Smith, **The Jesus of the Parables,** (Philadelphia: United Church Press, 1975), p. 105.
10. Ibid., p. 104.
11. Ronald S. Wallace, **Many Things in Parables,** (New York: Harper and Brothers, 1955), p. 106.
12. Ibid., p. 107.
13. J. Stanley Glen, **The Parables of Conflict in Luke,** (Philadelphia: Westminster, 1962), p. 51.
14. Ibid., p. 52.
15. Ibid., p. 52.
16. Ibid., p. 53.
17. Ibid., p. 53.
18. Ibid., p. 53.
19. Linnemann, op. cit., p. 55.
20. Ibid., p. 55.
21. A. E. Harvey, **Companion to the New Testament,** (Oxford: Oxford University Press, 1971), p. 253.
22. Ibid., p. 254.
23. Edmund Flood, **Parables of Jesus,** (New York: Paulist Press, 1971), p. 9.
24. Idea brought out in class discussion by students.
25. **Insights,** Vol. I, Number 16, June 25, 1974.
26. Hillyer Hawthorne Straton, **A Guide to the Parables of Jesus,** (Grand Rapids: Eerdmans, 1959), p. 112.
27. Brunner, op. cit., p. 57.

The
Home
Wrecker

3

THE PARABLE OF THE PRODIGAL SON
Luke 15:11-32

The parable of the Prodigal Son centers about the home, that place which creates a warm feeling within us all. It tells about a young man who was wild, rebellious and reckless. He ran away from home and wasted all his wealth, but he returned home and it was a better place because of him.

The parable also tells the story of a boy who was obedient, hard-working and honest. He stayed at home. But because of his smugness and self-centeredness, he ended up wrecking the home and it was a worse place because of him.

The Gospel shines through this story like a beacon of brilliant light in the darkest night, for the father loved them both — both the home waster and the home wrecker.

How to Title It

This parable has almost as many titles as it has interpretations. The traditional title is "The Prodigal Son" and reflects in most cases the moralistic approach to the parable. It is viewed as the story of a young man who runs away from home, lives an evil life, repents and returns home to his father. The lesson is directed to all evil persons. They should repent of their bad ways and come back home to God who will forgive them and reinstate them as his sons.

Many scholars like Emil Brunner would entitle it the parable of "The Two Sons."[1] They view it as a story which presents two basic relationships a person might have with God. Brunner says it is therefore "our story, yours and mine."[2] We are both, the son who ran away and the son who stayed at home. We are at times guilty of the younger son's sin of rebellion and at other times guilty of the pious sin of the elder son who finds no real joy when our erring brother finds his way back to God.

Wallace also sees it as the parable of two sons, one who **strayed** and one who **stayed**.[3] It is directed to the publicans and sinners who have lived a wasted life separated from God. It is also directed to the Pharisees who have wasted their lives keeping the commandments but failing to know the fatherly heart of God. His conclusion is that God has no preferences; he loves both the Pharisee and the publican.

J. Stanley Glen would also view it as a parable of two sons, each representing two conflicting bodies of people in Jewish society — the religious and the irreligious.[4] They are still with us today. The irreligious desire lawless freedom so they run away from God. However, their fling with freedom is disastrous, so they return and are surprised to find in the forgiving life of God the freedom which at first they thought could only be found by leaving God behind for atheism.[5]

The religious, feeling no responsibility for their brothers who are sinners, alienate themselves from God as much as if they had run away with the younger brother, the prodigal. So Glen agrees that the parable is the story of two prodigals.

Granskou entitles the parable "The Parable of the Elder Brother."[6] He focuses exclusively on the elder brother and is impressed with the fact that the father does not scold the elder son because of his snobbishness, smugness, and jealousy, but forgives him as he does the reckless wastefulness of the younger brother. Granskou sees in this the teaching that, "The ministry of Jesus to the poor is not a rejection of the righteous in favor of the sinner."[7] His conclusion is that God loves and seeks after all his children — the good as well as the bad.

Hunter[8] and Thielicke[9] would entitle this parable "The Waiting Father." Jeremias refers to it as the parable of "The Father's Love."[10] They take the position that Jesus is here depicting "the extravagant love of God — his sheer grace — to undeserving men."[11] They then warn against allegorization which would identify the father in the parable with God, and the danger of treating the parable as if it were an illustration of the total process of salvation. This is simply an example story which speaks of God's grace to sinners. It is the cross that presents to us the doctrine of the atonement — the return of sinners to God. In this parable we see only the compassionate love of God for sinners and his great joy at their return. We do not see a theological presentation of the **means** by which men come to salvation.

Thielicke summarizes the view that the father is the central figure in the story with these words, "The ultimate theme of this story, therefore, is not the prodigal son, but the father who finds us. The ultimate theme is not the faithlessness of men, but the faithfulness of God."[12]

One other approach needs to be noted and that is the interpretation of C. W. F. Smith, who sees the point of the parable in the **contrast**[13] between the attitude of the father and that of the older brother. The father represents the attitude of grace, the older brother that of the Law. The parable calls the listeners to form an opinion. Which attitude toward the returning sinner is to be commended and endorsed? To reject the attitude of the older son is to reject the critics of Jesus who attack his association with sinners. To accept the attitude of the father and share in his joy is to accept Jesus and his ministry to sinners.

Why the Younger Son Left Home

In the discussion above, the young man has been described in the traditional way as the boy who **ran** away from home. The story, however, does not support this description. The truth is he did not **run away;** he left in a very deliberate manner. He had undoubtedly thought about it for a long time. It was the result of a planned decision, not an impulse of the moment. The prodigal did not pack his bags and sneak out of the house under the cover of night like a Huckleberry Finn. No, he went to his father and told him what he had decided to do, and requested his share of the family inheritance.

Many interpreters believe that the prodigal left home because he was a young rebel; he wanted to be free from his father's domination. Theodore Parker Ferris from his historic pulpit describes the prodigal as "restless and adventurous."[14] At the very least it can be said that he was impatient and could not wait until his father died to get his share of the family estate.

The most favorable light that can be placed on the actions of the prodigal is that he was ambitious. Since according to law a farm-estate could not be broken up among the sons but given intact to the eldest son, the prodigal could have reasoned that there was no future on the farm for him. Jeremias points out that during the Diaspora about four million Jews migrated to more favorable living conditions in the great mercantile cities of other countries; therefore, the prodigal was not doing anything unusual.[15] Many young men in his day had done the same thing. They had asked for their inheritance of disposable property that did not belong directly to the farm, and they had gone into another country. Some of them later returned home with large fortunes.

Now we cannot know why the prodigal really left home. The story doesn't tell us. But neither does it give justification for assuming that what he did was immoral.

His leaving home should not be used as a symbolic action of sinfulness. He was not like Adam eating the forbidden fruit of disobedience. There is no indication that he is defying his father. He is being disrespectful, perhaps, but not rebellious as so many interpreters would have you believe.

Now it is true that his leaving home and his separation from his father created the possibility of his fall into evil ways. But he is presented in the story not so much as a moral sinner as a fool. He was a fool because of his failure to invest his inheritance wisely. His father had entrusted him with a portion of the family wealth and he wasted it. That is what "prodigal" means — "a waster." It is not synonymous with our understanding of the word "sinner." It was not his lack of moral respectability but his **irresponsibility** that is the tragic note of his experience in the far country.

Did Not Know His Father

Now whatever his real reason for leaving home, there is one aspect of this first part of the story that is often overlooked. The assumption is very clear that the father loved the younger son, but the tragedy is that apparently the boy didn't know it. He had lived in his father's house all his life and yet was never really convinced of his father's love. He believed his father to be a harsh stern disciplinarian — a man of justice and fairness, but not a man of compassion and forgiving love.

This is indicated by what went through the young man's mind when he came to himself and anticipated his return home. He did not see his father running forth with open arms to greet and forgive him. Rather he prepared himself for a reaction of anger. There was in his mind the strong possibility that his father would reject and refuse to accept him back into the household. So he planned to return, humble and penitent, and not ask to be received as a wayward son, but only as a hired worker.

There is an ancient Oriental legend which tells the story of a man who had a son who was wild and impetuous. He became involved with the ruffians of the village who persuaded him to join them in a robbery of his father's treasury house. After the robbery was over, his friends fled with the stolen treasure and left him to face the guilt of the crime alone. The young man was desperate. He was deserted by his friends and he had betrayed the trust of his father. But his greatest crime was that he had brought public dishonor on the family name. And in a culture where ancestors are worshiped and family integrity is a sacred trust, this was the worst wrong of all.

Broken and deeply repentant, he went to his father and begged forgiveness. Graciously it was granted. The father called all the members of the family together to celebrate the reconciliation and the return of his son. When all had enjoyed the banquet to the fullest, the father stood and lifted his cup of rice wine for a toast. But as the son drank deep the contents of his cup, he grabbed his throat and fell lifeless across the table. The son had been poisoned. The father with ceremonial dignity nodded to the guests. Each in turn graciously and politely bowed to the father as they silently left the banquet room. All was now put right. The son had paid the price of his pardon with poison. His honor had been restored. The family integrity and honor were reestablished. The unfortunate incident was closed.

Now the prodigal did not expect death as the demanded debt of his repentance, but this story does give us some insight into the Oriental mind, which places high priority on family honor and a son's respect for his father. The prodigal had no illusions of an easy reunion. He had offended his father and his family and was no longer worthy to be a son. Therefore his plan was to return and ask only to be a lowly servant.

The rest of the story also supports the fact that the son did not understand his father. And we shall see that this is also the tragedy of the elder brother. Perhaps it is also our tragedy. Whether we have strayed from, or stayed within the church, do we really know our God to be a loving and forgiving father?

The Father's Future Security

There is among the scholars disagreement as to the implications of the action of the son asking his father for his portion of the inheritance. Kenneth Bailey gives a very convincing case for the interpretation that in requesting his inheritance the son was actually wishing for his father's death. He quotes Levison: "There is no law or custom among Jew or Arab which entitles the son to a share of the father's wealth while the father is still alive."[16] He supports this with statements from the Bible and rabbinic teachings.

Eta Linnemann, on the other hand, gives an equally impressive presentation of authorities who claim the younger son did nothing wrong by his request, but had a legal and legitimate right to the disposable property that would one day be his.[17]

Whatever interpretation you place on the request of the son for his share of the property, the real point of insult to the father comes when the son takes the share of the property which is his and sells it. Speaking to this issue Jeremias wrotes, "The son obtains the right of possession . . . but the son does not acquire the right to dispose of the property."[18] If he does sell it, the purchaser cannot take possession of it until after his father's death. Therefore, it was not the asking for his share of the inheritance that struck the insulting blow against his father, but it was struck when he immediately sold his inheritance and turned it into ready cash so that he could go into the far country.

By this action he is not only breaking the law, but he is ignoring his responsibilty to his father's future security. All authorities agree that in the Hebrew culture, a son's responsibility for his father's future security was among the greatest of moral obligations. The Fourth Commandment states, "Honor thy father and mother." Some scholars are now pointing out that this means, "Care for them now and in their old age." This commandment was the "Social Security Act" of the Old Testament. Therefore, the younger son's disposing of his inheritance and turning it into cash to go into the far country was a blatant ignoring of his responsibility for his father's future well-being. The original listeners to this parable would on this basis have thought the son's actions to be a direct and deliberate insult to the father.

This brings us to the real point of this first action of the story. By selling his inheritance and thereby threatening his father's future security, the younger son had treated his father as if he were already dead. This was a tremendous insult to the father but the father does not rebuke or even beat his son. Apparently he sends him away with his blessing. So at the very beginning of the story we see an extraordinary expression of love on the part of the father. Right or wrong, legal or illegal, the father graciously gives the son what he requests and we thereby catch a vision of a very unusual father.

The Older Son

We often delegate the role of the elder son to the second half of the story, but Bailey points out that by assumption he plays a role in the division of the estate. According to Bailey, the listeners would have interpreted the action between the father and the younger son as a conflict within the family and they would have expected the older son to have stepped in and acted in the traditional role of reconciler.[19] Whenever there was a disagreement within a family a third party was expected to enter in and be arbitrator. This third person was always selected on the basis of the closeness of his relationship to each of the parties involved. In our parable this would indicate the responsibility was the elder son's. But there is no mention in the story that he assumes any responsibility for what is happening to his family, which might give some indication that hard feelings existed between the two brothers and prompted the younger brother to ask for his share of the inheritance to get away from an unhappy family situation.

It should not be overlooked that as Luke tells the story, "the father divided the property **between** his two sons." (verse 12b) This means that the elder son also benefited from his brother's request for his inheritance. We hear nothing of the elder brother's refusal to accept his share. Which again gives us a hint into the character of the elder brother long before we encounter him in the second half of the story.

The Community Alienated

So the younger son who has never gotten along with his older brother has now alienated himself from his father. And what is often overlooked — he has also succeeded in alienating himself from his friends in the village. The people of his hometown would have interpreted his actions of leaving home as a direct insult. They would have seen him as deciding that there was no future for an ambitious young man in this backward hicktown, so he is going into the big city with all its advantages for advancement.

In the time of our Lord, everyone lived in the closely knit unity of a village. Even farmers and vineyard keepers had their homes in the village and went out each morning to their fields. Therefore, whatever happened in the community involved and affected everybody in the village. So when the young prodigal packed his bag and headed for the big city, he succeeded in alienating himself from his father, his brother, and the whole community.

In the Far Country

In the far country our young hero succeeds in becoming a true prodigal by wasting his money in reckless living. It is interesting to note here that Luke does not say the young man wasted his money on prostitutes. This is left for the elder brother to say of him in the second half of the story, which again gives us a hint into the character and personality of the elder brother. Luke only establishes the fact that the young man wasted his money in the far country and became a prodigal.

In the eyes of the Pharisees who heard this story, however, the young man became more than a prodigal; he became a **sinner,** not in the moral sense because he played around with prostitutes, but in the religious sense, for he associated himself with Gentiles. In such a state he could not observe the Sabbath or follow any of the ritual rulings. This Luke makes clear as he includes the detail that the prodigal was sent out to a "farm to take care of the pigs." As the Jewish saying goes, "Cursed be the man who keeps swine."

In partial defense of the prodigal, it should be mentioned that the extent of degradation to which he sank was partly due to a factor beyond his control. A severe famine spread over the country. Under normal circumstances the prodigal might have found help or work in the local Jewish community, but in the time of famine such was not a practical option. So he was forced into the depths of degradation. He was guilty not only of wasting his father's wealth, but of apostasy to his father's faith. Jesus undoubtedly used these details to

ROUTING AND TRANSMITTAL SLIP

Date

TO: (Name, office symbol, room number, building, Agency/Post)	Initials	Date
1.		
2.		
3.		
4.		
5.		

Action	File	Note and Return
Approval	For Clearance	Per Conversation
As Requested	For Correction	Prepare Reply
Circulate	For Your Information	See Me
Comment	Investigate	Signature
Coordination	Justify	

REMARKS

Psalm 32.

—4 Lent—

Isa 12:1-6

Icon 1:18-31

G. Luke 15:1-3; 11-32.

DO NOT use this form as a RECORD of approvals, concurrences, disposals, clearances, and similar actions

FROM: (Name, org. symbol, Agency/Post)

Room No.—Bldg.

Phone No.

5041-102

OPTIONAL FORM 41 (Rev. 7-76)
Prescribed by GSA
FPMR (41 CFR) 101-11.206

add drama to the story and to heighten the loving forgiveness of the father.

Why Did He Return Home?

The prodigal did not turn his eyes homeward because he was homesick. Nor did he have a sudden conversion brought on by an evangelist preaching to him concerning his sinful life. His reasons for thinking about home were much more earthy.

First, **he ran out of funds.** He had squandered his inheritance and wasted his wealth in riotous, loose living. He spent his money on pleasures of the moment and now that the moment had passed, he was broke. If the funds had lasted, we can assume he would still be in the far country living it up. There is no indication that he didn't enjoy every minute of his playboy life. But his money was gone. He was broke and that was the first step in turning his eyes toward home.

Secondly, **he ran out of friends.** With the loss of funds came inevitably the loss of good-time friends. He was alone for the first time in his life. In his solitude he became aware of his estrangement from his father and his hometown friends. His loneliness also made him aware that he was alienated from himself. The unbearable conditions brought him to see his true destiny and the dramatic difference between what he was and what he could be. It also brought his attention to where he was and where he could be. He thought of home. No matter how unbearable conditions might be in his father's house, at least he would not be alone in the family. His brother may be pompous and pious, his father may be a harsh disciplinarian, but anything would be better than being alone with no companionship except the pigs.

The most obvious reason for his coming to himself and turning his eyes homeward is that **he ran out of**

food. A severe famine hit and he was hungry. We may get along in a limited way without funds and without friends, but a real crisis arises when we run out of food.

The story says he was so desperate that he would have eaten the carob pods which are berries of a wild shrub eaten only by pigs. They are bitter to the taste and without nourishment. Luke heightens his desolation by adding, ". . . but no one gave him any."

So the real dramatic turning point of the story was his stomach pangs. It was not his conscience. It was not his moral awareness that he had done wrong by wasting his father's money. It was not his religious convictions that he was failing to observe the Sabbath and the ritualistic rules of his faith. It was the simple earthy drive of his physical body. He was hungry. The only thing he could think about was that his father's hired workers had more than they could eat and he was starving to death. He thought to himself, "It is better to be a slave and eat than to be a free man and starve." Hunger has driven many a man home and to places not so desirable.

Many moralistic preachers have dealt with this text and focused in on the idea of repentance as being the basic motivation that drove the young man home to beg forgiveness of his father. They conclude that we should preach the Law and convict men of their sins. Scare people with the threat of hell and the eternal punishment of death and you will drive people home to God in repentance and tears. This may be true. However, such a sermon is not justifiable on the basis of this parable. The young man was brought to the realization that he had made a mistake by leaving home and had failed miserably in the management of his funds and choice of friends. But it was not the Law, or the spouting of pious phrases and platitudes that broke him. It was hunger.

The Prodigal's Plan

The surprising thing about this story is that the

prodigal is not really presented as being truly repentant in the far country. He is still the same self-reliant and independent person he was at the beginning of the story. Luke indicates this by not using the theological word for repentance but a much weaker word which means "changed his mind, or his opinion," or it might even be translated "reconsidered his position." The picture the parable presents is that he sat himself down and took stock of his situation to see how he could get out of the mess he had gotten himself into. The King James version says, ". . . he came to himself." The Good News version is better: "He came to his senses." The implication is that he is not concerned with changing himself, which would be a repentant attitude, but changing the conditions or circumstances of his life. For this he needs a plan. Suddenly the perfect plan comes to him. He knows there is no chance he can return home as if nothing had happened. He has given up all rights to be a son, so he will go back and be a servant in his father's house. He says, "I will get up and go to my father and say, 'Father, I have sinned against God and against you. I am no longer fit to be called your son; treat me as one of your hired workers.' " This self-effacement is part of his plan; it is not the sincere confession of a repentant person, as we will see later on. This is a picture of a young man who has been broken but now is getting up on his own two feet to work out a very careful plan for his own salvation. His desperate circumstances have not gotten the better of him. He has come "to the senses" and he is going to be a winner despite it all. This is not a repentant young man; this is a clever and determined young man.

Oesterley[20] is helpful here, for he points out that there are three options for servanthood open to him. First there is the **bondsman,** who was a slave but held in high esteem and treated as a member of the family. The second classification of servanthood was a **slave-lower class**, who was a subordinate to the bondsman. And the

78

third classification was a **hired-servant,** who was a free man. He did not belong to the estate. He was an independent wage-earner. This is the option the prodigal chose.

Now the face-saving, clever plan of the prodigal becomes obvious. The same self-determined, independent spirit of the prodigal comes through as in the beginning of the story. He will earn a wage and fulfill some of his moral obligations by paying back a portion of the money he owes to his father's future security. He will still be a free man. He will not have to live in his father's house and suffer the humiliation of eating his brother's food. He will solve his own problem and save himself by his own sweat, hard work and personal labor. He wants no handouts from his father or his brother. He will do it on his own. As J.D.M. Derrett points out, the prodigal son wants no grace.[21] The young man has not repented; he is the same freedom-loving, self-reliant, independent cuss as he was at the beginning of the story.

The Prodigal's Return

The clever plan of the prodigal to work out his own salvation will take care of the relationship to his father and his brother, but he still has to cope with the alienation of the town. Here Kenneth Bailey is helpful as he describes the situation. The prodigal son returns to face "the slander of a whole town and certainly the gathering of an unfriendly mob. As soon as the prodigal reaches the edge of the village he will be subjected to taunting chants and many other verbal and perhaps even physical abuse."[22]

The father is aware of this, and he too has a plan. Then follows one of the most heart-moving dramas in all of scripture. The crowd has gathered. The son approaches the village steeling his nerves for a hostile encounter with the villagers. His worst fears are realized; as he arrives at the village the townspeople stand gathered as one in an angry mob. The situation is explosive. Some hold clubs, others pick up stones, all raise their voices to jeer at him. Then suddenly bursting forth from the angry gathering his father comes running. For an elderly man to run is not only undignified, but humiliating. The villagers cannot believe what they are witnessing; they stop in their tracks, their voices fall to silence. The father rushes up to his son with open arms and covers him with kisses. To the stunned eyes of the villagers, this demonstration of affection means forgiveness and reconciliation. They drop their clubs, embarrassed, and let the stones slip from their hands to the ground. Their feelings are softened and they stand amazed in the presence of so great a love.

But if the villagers are stunned, the prodigal is even more so. He does not follow through on his well-developed plan to save himself. He is overwhelmed by his father's expression of love, and surrenders to it. His pride and self-reliance melt into tears of joy as he stands embraced by free grace. He tries to confess. He says, "Father, I have sinned against God and against you. I am no longer fit — to be — called — your — son." Then he stops. He never finishes. His carefully devised plan is forgotten in the presence of unexpected, unbelievable love.

And here is the profound insight of the parable. What actually works the change in this young man and makes a new man of him is not the experience of poverty, forsaken friends, or near starvation in the far country, but the expression of the unmerited love and forgiveness of the father. It is at this point that the son is converted, changed about, and becomes a new person. The prodigal thought the answer to all his problems was a plan to work out his own salvation, but he was wrong. It was pure grace, and pure grace alone, that was his only means to true salvation and restoration.

Now the son knows that his great wrong doing was not the loss of his inheritance, but the fact that he had willingly separated himself from a father who loved him more than life itself. And that broken relationship could not be bought or earned by good works; it could only be given by free grace.

Once more, divine grace has triumphed and has shown to us the folly of all our efforts to save ourselves.

The Marks Of Sonship

The father performs three symbolic acts to reassure his son of his acceptance. First, the robe is placed on him indicating that he is an honored guest. A ring is placed on the prodigal's finger as a symbol of authority. It was a sign that he was still his father's son. He thought he had lost his inheritance in a far country — wasted it away in riotous living. But to his surprise, he discovered his inheritance was much more than money; it was sonship and that could never be lost. Sonship had always been his and it was still his. Sonship cannot be spent, or wasted, or thrown away, even in a far country. We may deny it. We may attempt to run away from it and forget it, but a son is still a son no matter how far he separates himself from his father.

Then finally shoes are placed on the young man's feet as a sign and symbol that he is not a slave but a free man. The father did not want a hired-servant-son; he had one of those already in the person of the elder brother. He did not want a slave who worked **for** him, but a son who received **from** him.

So with the robe and the ring and the shoes the father pronounces three blessings upon his son: honor, authority, and freedom. The three undeniable assertions of sonship. Ironic, isn't it, that the very things the prodigal had run away from home to find he really had all the time right in his own back yard?

But even more important than honor, authority and freedom, the son received a new understanding of his father. He literally saw his father for the first time in his life and discovered that he was a father of forgiving love. His father was not a man of the Law but of love. Not first a man of justice but of grace.

The feast which followed, with its satisfying enjoyment of the fatted calf and the hours of celebration, was nothing compared with the hunger that was satisfied deep down in the very being of this young man as he discovered his father's love. Hunger for fun and freedom might have driven this young man away from his home, and the hunger for food might have driven him back, but in his father's arms he found his greatest hunger satisfied. He now knew his father's love, and in and by that knowledge he was literally born again to new life.

The Elder Prodigal

The elder son is outside his father's house. He is not in a far country; he is in the fields. In every sense, however, he is as separated from his father as much as the younger son was in the far country. Rebellious freedom separated the prodigal from his father. A slave-like approach to obedience separates the elder son from his father. Both boys failed in their own ways to understand their father's love.

Apparently the elder brother is not notified of his brother's return. It may have been that the father figured that the elder brother would be so upset as to do something foolish and rash. He might even try to prevent the banquet. What happens, however, is just about as bad.

As the elder boy returns from the fields and approaches his home, he hears music and dancing. Eta Linnemann points out that the feast must have been well underway by this time, as dancing usually follows a festive meal.[23] The elder son refuses to go into the house. Bailey comments here that custom requires his presence as elder sons usually act as the major domo of a feast and make sure that everyone enters into the spirit of the party and has a good time.[24] In this case, just the opposite happens and the elder son refuses to enter into the festivities.

Then the story tells us that the father goes out to him and begs him to come in. It is interesting that here the action of the father toward the elder son is a repetition of the father's action toward the young son. It is the father that goes out to the son. Then follows one of the most surprising scenes of the parable so far as the original listeners were concerned. The older brother openly attacks his father in public, accusing him of a lack of fatherly concern. To understand the dramatic impact of this part of the story, we need to remember that houses in the days of our Lord were not closed boxes but open, airy structures. The inside was not closed off by continuous walls from the outside, but was separated only by open, spacious arches so that anything that happened immediately outside the house was in easy hearing and viewing of everybody inside the house. The exchange between the elder son and the father was therefore witnessed by all the guests.

Everyone could see that the son was angry. He shouted at his father, "Look, all these years I have worked like a slave for you, and not once did I disobey an order of yours. What have you given me? Not even a goat for me to have a feast with **my** friends." He sneered out the words "my friends," and this was a direct insult to the gathered guests. It implied that the people attending this feast were friends of the father and of the younger son; they were not **his** friends. Then he went on, "But this son of yours . . ." Note he does not say "my brother," but "this son of yours." And then he adds, ". . . wasted all your property on prostitutes." The guests were shocked, for such accusations against a member of the family are never made in public. Every action and statement of the older son is highly improper and extremely insulting to his father. In a sense, what the older brother was doing was more radically humiliating to the father than the act of the young son in running away from home.

The elder son could have waited until after the party and the guests had gone home before attacking his father, but he chooses to humiliate his father publicly. The listeners certainly expected the father to explode and punish his son on the spot for his insolence. At the very least he should have slapped the boy across the face and ordered him into the feast or commanded his servants to take him back out into the fields until his temper cooled off. But the father did just the opposite. He talked gently with him. "My son, everything I have is yours." The guests could not believe what they were seeing and hearing. The insulted and humiliated father is pleading with a son who has publicly disgraced him. But if they were moved, the elder son was not. Unexpected, extraordinary love had changed the younger son and converted him, but there is no indication that it changed the elder. The story ends and we are not permitted to see how it all eventually turned out.

Perhaps this is because each of us needs to complete the story for ourselves. Jesus told this parable to elder-son-type people, people who were within the household of God and who were refusing to celebrate our Lord's mission to sinners and outcasts. And can we not see ourselves in the shoes of the elder son? How often we refuse the message of free grace, always insisting that people must do something to merit salvation — even if it is just believing in Christ. We are convinced that the kingdom really belongs to those who stay at home in the father's house as obedient children and labor diligently in the father's fields before they can deserve the feast of the fatted calf we call salvation.

We cry out "Cheap Grace" whenever free, unmerited forgiveness and love are mentioned. But don't you see that what this parable is saying is that God wants **sons** and not **hired-servants** in his kingdom? If we work for our salvation, if we do meritorious deeds such as lengthy confessions for past sins, or public proclamation of strong conviction and belief, then we are working for our redemption as hired servants, and salvation becomes not a gift of grace but a wage earned by good works. Then when Christ goes to a cross there is nothing decisive that he can do for us, or give to us, for we have worked out our salvation; we have borne our own crosses of obedience and repentance and do not need him.

In the parable both sons were wrong. Both in their own way felt they could earn their place in their father's house. The younger thought he could work as a hired servant and pay his father back for the mistakes he had committed. The elder son thought he could work as an obedient son and therefore deserve an honored place in his father's house. Both were wrong.

The difference, the decisive difference, is that the younger son, when encountering the extraordinary love of his father, changed, surrendered to free grace. The elder son, experiencing the same free grace through forgiving love, did not change, but defended his meritorious right to a place in his father's house. Where do we stand?

Celebration

This parable also says something very definite about forgiveness. It presents us with forgiveness not simply as something promised and given but as something to be celebrated. It is not just a doctrine talked about, explained and proclaimed, but something we are to experience and participate in. The younger son came to know his father's love through the experience of his forgiveness. The elder son had the opportunity to know his father's love through the forgiveness of his brother. Both are ways in which we come to know God and experience his love for us — as we experience his forgiveness personally, and as we share in the experience of our brother's being forgiven.

The elder brother was a prodigal because he wasted the opportunity to celebrate his brother's forgiveness. As the story so graphically phrases it, "He refused to go in." He would not enter into the celebration of his brother's forgiveness.

Now this is precisely the failure of the Christian Church today. Again and again in the front lines of faith we fail to be a community within the world where sinful men and women might come in and experience within our fellowship the forgiveness which our doctrines proclaim.

We hear a great deal today about telling the story of the Gospel. We open up lines of communication between the church and the world. We enter into dialogue with architect and artist, university professor and factory worker. We write new liturgies in everyday language. We struggle in conference, committees, bull sessions, and buzz groups to make our message clear and understandable. But all this is "prodigal effort" if when the world listens and understands and comes into the church, it fails to experience the forgiving love we have gone to such pains to communicate clearly.

Talk is not enough. Words must take on the warm-blooded flesh of human experience. That is why God became incarnate, and that is why our Lord gathered about himself a little band of faithful men and women. He wanted to establish a fellowship where what he said might become incarnate in the community.

Today that fellowship is the church and our challenge is not "go to church" but "be the church" — become that place where what God says is experienced. But how often we fail. Sinners do not find the fellowship of forgiveness within our midst. Like the elder son, we refuse to "enter in" and celebrate the return of the prodigals to their father's home. We view the church as a club for the righteous "right guys" rather than as a hospital for those injured by life.

We fail as a fellowship because we prefer to intellectualize our faith rather than to actualize it. We make of our churches places where we come to hear someone else talk to us about God. We forget that faith is not something taught but caught. Faith is contagious when lived out in our daily lives. It is irresistable when we share it with others.

In most cases the people of God are the last to forget and love unwanted brothers. We are the first to gossip and judge, but the last to forgive. The average prodigal finds more acceptance, comfort, care and concern in the local bar than in the corner church.

Too often when the prodigal returns home we act like the elder brother. We withdraw into our pious shells and look down our moralistic noses and make wrongdoers feel that they are not good enough to share our holy fellowship. When we do this we do not have a church; we have a social club. We have only buildings built with human hands — all stained glass and glittering brass — signifying nothing except our own false vanity and empty hypocrisy. We live out our lives like the elder brother, wrecking the church we call our home.

If the house of God is ever to become the home of God, it will be when we enter the celebration of the returned prodigal. He is our brother and our father's son. He was lost and is now found. He was dead and is alive. That is enough for even God to celebrate and find joyful. Can we refuse to enter into so great a joy?

Notes

1. Emil Brunner, **Sowing and Reaping**, (Richmond, Va.: John Knox, 1946). p. 34.
2. Ibid., p. 37.
3. Ronald S. Wallace, **Many Things in Parables,** (New York: Harper and Brothers, 1955), p. 61.
4. J. Stanley Glen, **The Parables of Conflict in Luke,** (Philadelphia: Westminster, 1962), p. 26.

5. Ibid., p. 33.
6. David M. Granskou, **Preaching on the Parables,** (Philadelphia: Fortress, 1972), p. 95.
7. Ibid., p. 96.
8. Archibald M. Hunter, **The Parables Then and Now,** (Philadelphia: Westminster, 1971), p. 59.
9. Helmut Thielicke, **The Waiting Father,** (New York: Harper and Brothers, 1959), pp. 17-40.
10. Joachim Jeremias, **The Parables of Jesus,** (New York: Charles Scribner's Sons, 1955), p. 103.
11. Hunter, op. cit., p. 60.
12. Thielicke, op. cit., p. 29.
13. Charles W.F. Smith, **The Jesus of the Parables,** (Philadelphia: United Church Press, 1975), p. 77.
14. Theodore Parker Ferris, Sermon preached in Trinity Church Boston, May 21, 1967.
15. Joachim Jeremias, **Rediscovering the Parables,** (New York: Charles Scribner's Sons, 1966), p. 102.
16. Kenneth E. Bailey, **Poet and Peasant,** (Grand Rapids: Eerdmans, 1976), p.162.
17. Eta Linnemann, **Jesus of the Parables,** (New York: Harper and Row, 1964), pp. 73-81.
18. Jeremias, op. cit., p. 101.
19. Bailey, op. cit., p. 168.
20. W.O.E. Oesterley, **The Gospel Parables in the Light of Their Jewish Background,** (London: SPCK, 1936), p. 186.
21. J. Duncan Derrett, **Mosaic Law in the New Testament,** (London: Darton, Longman and Todd, 1970), pp. 56-74.
22. Bailey, op. cit., p. 181.
23. Linnemann, op. cit., p. 79.
24. Bailey, op. cit., p. 194.

88

No
Little
Bo
Peep
Theology

4

THE PARABLE OF THE LOST SHEEP
Luke 15:1-10

Most of us remember a little girl from our childhood
days named Little Bo Peep. According to her familiar
nursery rhyme:
Little Bo Peep, lost her sheep
and doesn't know where to find them.
Leave them alone, and they'll come home
wagging their tails behind them.
Now there is a theology here, a theology that deals with
an issue central in the New Testament, **lostness.** The
theology of Little Bo Peep is non-involvement, hands off,
don't touch the sinners. This was the theology of the
Pharisees at the time of Jesus. They pigeon-holed everybody who didn't act the way they thought they should, or
looked the way they wanted them to, and labeled them
sinners, publicans and outcasts. They were the dirt of
Jewish society, so the Pharisees contemptuously and
ceremonially washed their hands of them.
It is important to understand what the Pharisees
really meant when they used the word "sinner." Today
we think of the term in an exclusively moral context. But
in the days of Jesus it had strong social connotations.
Jeremias states that " 'sinner' had a two-fold meaning.
First of all it meant 'people who lead an immoral life
(e.g.) adulterers, swindlers,' and secondly 'people who
followed a dishonorable occupation ... custom officers,
tax collectors, shepherds, donkey drivers, peddlers, and
tanners.' "[1]
For the Pharisees a sinner was anyone who did not
attend the temple and observe the ritualistic rules of
Jewish piety. This included those who lived immoral

lives and refused to abide by the laws. It also included the peasants who found that their poverty prevented them from attending the services of the temple. They had to work to eat and this meant they had neither the time or the opportunity to observe all the ritualistic rules and regulations that the religious specialists had devised. The publicans were classified by the Pharisees alongside of sinners because of their occupation. They gathered taxes and customs duties for the hated Romans and were regarded as contemptible traitors. So the sinners outraged the Pharisees' moral respectability and the publicans offended their national pride.

Jesus, however, ignored the condemnation of the Pharisees and sought out sinners. He was not concerned with the labels society placed outwardly upon them; he was interested in their inward potential. The disciples which he called to be his followers were in his eyes not just bad-tempered, foul-mouthed fishermen from the Sea of Galilee or backward, ignorant commoners, but men with a great destiny, willing to die witnessing to his words. Zacchaeus was not just a piece of the corrupt establishment driven by curiosity up a tree; he was a man ripe for the new life. The woman taken in adultery was not just one more case history of the shocking decline in morals, but a person capable of responding to a love that wanted not to use her but to renew her. The tax collectors and sinners who flocked to hear him were not only cheats, extortioners and general contributors to soaring crime rates and sinking moral standards; they were the chosen children of God, who were by circumstances or willful choice separated from their father-God. It made no difference to Jesus if they were rich or poor, smart or dumb, weak or strong, religious or irreligious, without or outside the Law — they were lost from God and that is all Jesus needed to know.

In the practical situation, however, it turned out that the lower classes were more receptive of him and therefore he spent more time with them. Jesus had a much broader concept of sinner than had the Pharisees but he apparently chose to associate with the poor, not by deliberate plan but simply because they were the ones who received and listened to him.

There is no evidence in the New Testament that Jesus came only to the lower class citizens of Jewish society. He numbered among his followers those who were rich and influential as well as the poverty stricken. His closest friends outside the band of disciples were Mary, Martha and their brother Lazarus. They may not have been considered rich, but they were comfortable middle class. Joseph of Arimathea, who provided for our Lord a tomb, was by any standard a wealthy man. So it was not a deliberate assertion of Jesus but the accusation of the Pharisees that labeled him exclusively the friend of publicans and sinners.

A Two-Way Street

Marcus Dods makes an interesting observation that is frequently overlooked by interpreters of this parable. He points out that Jesus' relationship with sinners was a two-way street. Jesus not only went to sinners, but they came to him. If the Pharisees were surprised and shocked to see Jesus associating with publicans and sinners, they must have been equally surprised that outcasts sought after and longed to talk with Jesus. It was not usual that sinners would choose to consort with a man who publicly claimed to be sent from God.

Dods puts it this way: "Men whom society had branded as outcasts and who flung back on society a scorn as contemptuous as its own; men who had long since abandoned all belief in goodness, and who delighted in showing their disbelief were not ashamed even in the public streets, to own to him their sin and to supplicate his mercy."[2]

The obvious reason why these dissolute and lawless characters responded to Jesus was that he did not shrink from them as had other religious teachers. He spoke to them on their own level as one of them. He gave them a word of hope in their hopeless condition. But even more, it was the way in which he did it. He did not take a superior attitude toward them. He did not lecture to them or quote scriptures at them. He did not judge, condemn and threaten them with hell and damnation. He did not present to them minute directives for their daily lives in the form of rules and regulations. No, he spoke to them of forgiveness, turning one's back on the past and starting again a new way of living. He simply said, "Go and sin no more."

All of their lives they had heard how bad they were. They had been branded and marked as undesirables and the treatment they received from good and respectable people convinced them this was so. Then Jesus comes to them, accepts them, eats with them, shows concern and that he truly cares for them. They were shocked as much as the Pharisees, but they responded because for the first time in their lives they felt that they meant something to somebody, and the greatest surprise of all was that this somebody, according to Jesus himself, claimed to be sent from the Holy God their Creator-Father.

Now this should say something to us. We are not just called to serve sinners, but to serve them in a specific way — to serve them without destroying their dignity as persons. Evangelism is a two-way street. We need not only want to go to them; they must want to come to us because of the way we relate and treat them when they do come.

Judgment, condemnation, warnings, and threats are not the ways to convince people of their need for Christ. We must first bring them to realize we are their friends and are honestly concerned for their well being. They are not new members we need to fulfill our evangelistic quota, nor to enlarge our church rolls; they are people we would like to have as friends and share with them our common Lord.

So Jesus comes with a love and a concern for all people as persons no matter what their status in society. But he comes seeking first those who are lost, those who are living second rate lives because of their separation from God. This the Pharisees did not understand. They could see only that he claimed to be a teacher sent from God but he associated with people far beneath the social status of a rabbi. He claimed to be a holy man, but he chose as his companions unholy people. It just didn't make sense to the Pharisees. In fact, they believed he was threatening the religious and social stability. This is the real irony of it all; in the minds of the Pharisees sin was not the disturbing problem in God's world — Jesus was. As long as sinners knew their place and stayed in it, society was at peace and all well. Like Little Bo Peep, the Pharisees preferred and practiced the theology, "Let them alone!"

The Lost

The text makes it quite clear that Jesus told the parable of the Lost Sheep as a rebuttal to the Pharisees' accusation that he was associating with publicans and sinners. It is very important to note that Jesus did not tell a story about a sinner who repents and returns to God. He does not use the word "sinner" at all in his story. It is about a sheep — an ordinary sheep lost, sought for, and found. It is not about the **black sheep** of the flock. It is not a **bad** sheep anymore than the ninety-nine were **good** sheep.[3] The idea of goodness and badness does not enter into the plot of the story. Even the rejoicing at the end of the story was not over a **repentant sheep;** it was over a found sheep.

So Jesus is saying in effect to the Pharisees that he is

associating with these people not because they are moral and religious sinners as the Pharisees classify them, but he seeks them out because they are lost. Christ is not overlooking or condoning their badness; he is concerned with something more basic and important to him — the fact that these people are lost, separated from God their father.

We tend to think of the word "sinner" and "the lost" as synonymous. When we hear the word "lost" we are apt to think of **lost souls,** the Last Judgment and hell. Hugh Martin, however, states very strongly that the "lost" cannot be translated as "the damned." This is not at all what Jesus is talking about. Martin goes on to define "lostness" as the state of those who are "lost to divine service and fellowship, they are not in their proper place, or fulfilling their true end in life of serving God and enjoying him forever."[4] The lost are not those who are immoral, evil or bad but the lost are those who are separated from God and therefore cannot fulfill the potential of their personhood. Now it is true that because they are lost and separated from God they fall into evil ways. They break the law and commit evil deeds but this is the result of their lostness and not the cause of it. The lost, from Jesus' point of view, are those who are not what God intends them to be. They are those who are failing to fulfill their God-intended destiny. Therefore, the task of Jesus is not to **reform the sinner** but **restore the separated.**

Now this is important if we are to understand the parable, for it is not a picture of how unbelieving sinners are converted and brought into the church, but how God's own who are lost to him are brought back to him. This would direct the concern of God not just to sinners and publicans but to the Pharisees as well. People can be lost inside the Law as well as outside of it. Therefore, Jesus tells his story about a sheep — not a bad sheep who willfully runs away from the flock but a common, ordinary sheep who thoughtlessly nibbles his way farther and farther away from the flock until he is separated and lost. He is not guilty of a breach of the Law; he is not guilty of anything. He is simply lost and needs to be found or else, as night falls, he will die in his helpless condition.

Love Of The Many

It is also important to see that there is within these parables of lostness an assumed relationship between creation and redemption. In the religious thinking of the Jews the ultimate goal toward which everything moved was the great Messianic banquet which would be held at the end of time. God would be sitting at his table and all his faithful children would be gathered around him. This was the final hope of God from the beginning, but sin and man's rebellion entered in and God's created children were separated from him. The sacred history of Israel was God's great effort to restore his family. So the redemptive process becomes part of the creative process. What God ultimately desires to create is an obedient and loving family. The picture of a finished creation would be all of God's children gathered about him as one big happy family. Now it is true that the Jews had narrowed the concept of God's children until it meant for them only the Jewish race, but this does not destroy the basic revelatory truth that God's basic concern is for the corporate family of his children.

Therefore, the concern for the fellowship creates the concern for the individual person. The story of the lost sheep should not be seen as a concern only for a lost individual but in the broader sense as a concern for the completed fellowship. God searches for the lost in order that his family might be complete.

A little girl was once asked by her Sunday school teacher to explain the 23rd Psalm, and with profound simplicity she said, "What it really means is that everybody is somebody to God."

There is no implication within the parable that the shepherd loves the lost more than the ninety-nine. Rather, it is the love for the ninety-nine and his desire to make his flock complete that drives the shepherd forth to search for the one. Therefore, the more love strains itself to restore the one, the more we realize the great love for the ninety-nine. We must not fall into the trap of so many hearers of this parable who worry about the fact that the ninety-nine are neglected in favor of the one. It is God's love for the ninety-nine that makes his love reaction radical to save and restore the one.

Radical, Aggressive Love

This parable calls for a mature view of the aggressive nature of divine love. We are brought up on a sentimental, tender concept of love. Love is gentle, patient and passive. And this is true, but this parable points out that love is also aggressive, ambitious and active. It is not the placid, indifferent love of Little Bo Peep towards her sheep; rather love boldly strikes out to find those who are lost.

When the story tells us about a man who leaves his flock and goes out after the one that is lost, it presents a radical concept of love. Jeremias points out that it is a ridiculous reaction; no shepherd would leave his flock to the mercy of wild animals and thieves to search for one lost lamb.[5] There are many answers that can be given to Jeremias's comment, as we shall see later on in the discussion. However, at this point in our understanding of the parable, this is not the real issue.

The parable shows a very emotional, illogical reaction of love. Love does not survey the situational problem and come to a logical and reasonable solution. This is a story of how love reacts spontaneously to an emergency situation.

Off the coast of Woodshole, Massachusetts, a storm suddenly arose and a mother rushed to the beach shouting that her young son was out there in a small boat fishing. Immediately a group of men climbed into a boat and moved out into the churning waters to rescue that one child. One of the village women said, "It seems so foolish that so many men should risk their lives for one child." To which her friend came back, "Would you feel the odds were wrong if you were that child?"

The odds of the parable, ninety-nine to one, are meant only as a dramatic device of the storyteller to heighten the emergency aspect of the story. And that is the key to understanding the plot of the story — it is an emergency situation. Policemen, firemen, emergency squads do this all the time. There are always situations in which the many are risked for the sake of the few.

Parents under normal circumstances love all their children equally. They do not intentionally neglect some for others. They try to treat all their children the same. But if one child were to become sick, or get into serious trouble, then that is an emergency situation and the parents neglect the rest of the children to care for that one sick or troubled child.

So this parable is not a picture of how love ordinarily acts, but how love acts in an emergency. The Lord is exaggerating and presenting an illogical reaction to the lost. But as a storyteller he is doing this for a purpose. Our Lord believed that his coming created a crisis situation. The Kingdom of God had come in him. The time was short and therefore God was moving in on his world, to seek out and search for and find the lost. This is the amazing and radical reaction of love in the time of an emergency.

Jesus began his ministry telling his parents that he must be about his father's business. Now he is showing by parable and deed what his father's business is — to find the lost, and to find them now!

The Shock Of The Pharisees

The story of the Lost Sheep, rather than convincing the Pharisees that Jesus was right associating with sinners, only succeeded in shocking them and alienating them even more. They were first of all shocked by the fact that the story implies that God suffers a loss when the sinner is separated from him. To the Pharisees this was an entirely new light on the character of God.[6] They viewed God as a stern disciplinarian enforcing his will by compulsion and punishing anyone who was disobedient and strayed from him. God was totally self-sufficient and needed nothing, for he was everything. Then to hear that the lostness of the sinner was God's loss and that he suffered as well as the sinner in this state of separation was inconceivable to the Pharisees.

And is this not difficult for us to believe, that God suffers over every trouble and disaster which befalls us?

A young father seeing his son struck and killed by a passing car cried out, "Where was God when my son was killed?" His pastor gave the only answer possible, "He was in the same place that he was when his son was killed." God does not intervene or intrude into every case of need our cause-and-effect world thrusts upon us, but this does not mean he is unaffected. God is concerned and truly cares what happens to us but in his wisdom he knows that too much divine intervention destroys human ingenuity and makes of us puppets rather than persons. Therefore, he holds back his hand and suffers with us, waiting until that day when he can turn all of our suffering into joy.

Now this compassionate concern of God for his children the Pharisees had completely left out of their understanding of the personhood of God. And that is why when Jesus tells a story about God's love and concern for the lost and says that God experiences a sense of deep loss in their separation from him, the Pharisees were dumb-founded.

The Pharisees were also shocked to hear that God was not only concerned for the lost, but that he was **so concerned** that he left what he was doing and went out in search of them. The parable at first sounded familiar to the Pharisees. They had heard the rabbis tell stories about a coin and a sheep that was lost and diligently searched for. But these stories were told in the synagogues and used by the rabbis to illustrate how man should strive to find God.[7] As a shepherd searches for a lost sheep and a woman searches for her misplaced coin, so man should search and find, please, and be obedient to God. Jesus had reversed the meaning of the stories. He had literally turned them upside-down. Christ was saying that the seeker was not man but God. And even more shocking, God was searching not for a good and honest man, but for sinners, the riff-raff, the dirty and the diseased, the socially undesirable.

Today we are bombarded on billboards and bumper stickers with the slogan, "I found it." Now the intention of this movement is undoubtedly sincere, but the theology is seriously confused. The implication is that we search out and find God. This was the theology of the Pharisees which Jesus so energetically attacked. The radical revelation of Jesus was that God searches for and finds us. The slogan born in the heart of the New Testament is not, "I found it, but "He found me." If the "I Found It" theology were true then Jesus would have told a parable about a little lost lamb who searched wildly through the wilderness until he found a shepherd.

The greatest shock, however, to the Pharisees is what the parable said concerning repentance. The Pharisees and the Jewish thinkers in general valued repentance very highly. They took for granted that a truly repentant man would be accepted by God. Levison, in his book about the background of the parables, goes so far as to say, "It is even true to say that he (the repentant man) was counted more worthy than a righteous person."[8]

102

Eta Linnemann very effectively shows how seriously the Pharisees take repentance by telling the following story based on an old Jewish legend:

"Nahum of Gimso, the pious teacher, was one day driving three asses, laden with bread and fruits, to the house of study. While he was following the beasts in the midday heat, more asleep than awake, a sick beggar deformed with ulcers and half-dead of hunger, came up to him and asked for some food.

"Nahum had never refused a beggar, but the heat of the day made him lazy, and he answered crossly, 'Just wait until I have found something for you.' With reluctant feet he followed the beast that had gone ahead, and began bad-temperedly to grope about in the panniers. But while he was still feeling about aimlessly, there struck his ear a weak and yet terribly urgent sigh, and when he turned around, the beggar lay stretched out dead in the sand.

"How quick were Nahum's hands to take the bread and fruit out of the pannier, how swiftly his feet hurried back! He implored the dead man to eat, he threw himself on his ulcerated body to bring him back to life. But it was all in vain. Then Nahum cried to God and said, 'Lord of the world! Through my laziness a man's life has been lost! O ease my grief and punish me. May the feet that were slow to bring help to the needy become lame, the hands that were so negligent to serve him wither up, the eyes that looked askance at his need go blind, and my body bear his illness. Lord of the world, so punish me in this life and in my body, that thou punish me not in the next life and in my soul!" From that day on Nahum was sick. His feet went lame, his hands withered, his eyes went blind, and his body was covered with sores.

"Once Rabbi Akiba, his pupil, visited him, and when he saw him lying, so wasted in his bed-sheets, he cried out for sorrow and said, 'Woe is me that I must see you like this, you pious man!'

"But Nahum smiled and said, 'Blessed are you, Akiba, that you can see me so, for this is a sign of grace to me, that God demands my sins from me in this life and in my body, and leaves me unharmed in the next life and in my soul.' "[9]

This graphically illustrates with what great seriousness the Pharisees looked upon repentance. And what was so essential to their doctrine was that sinners should take the initiative. Only then when they had a repentant and submissive attitude, only when they came home "wagging their tails behind them," could they be welcomed by both God and man.[10]

It is easy to see, therefore, why the parable of the Lost Sheep upset the Pharisees. Jesus had reversed not only the origin but the order of repentance. Rather than repentance being the first thing, the condition and the requirement for forgiveness and its accompanying fellowship with God, it became the result. And the origin instead of being man's responsibility — something he must initiate — became an event of God's coming to man. The message which Jesus proclaimed at the beginning of his ministry now really became, "You **can** repent, because the Kingdom of God has come among you."

This radical reorientation of the Pharisees' well-established doctrine of repentance was undoubtedly one of the major reasons why they declared, "This man blasphemes against the Holy God," and led to their final indictment, "Crucify him!"

The Little Bo Peep theology, "Let them alone," did not apply to Christ. This young man was too dangerous to be "let alone;" they must rid themselves and Jerusalem of this black-hearted sheep. He was a sheep in wolf's clothing. He was no son of God; he was a chief sinner against God.

Not A Missionary Text

The parable of the Lost Sheep did not convince the

Pharisees, but it has over the years convinced the church that Jesus has given in the story a directive for great missionary endeavors. The task of the church has been seen, in the light of this parable, as a call to seek the "lost souls," to convert and save the pagans and the unbelievers of the world. In fact, the dramatic detail that ninety-nine are neglected has suggested to some homileticians that ninety-nine percent of the church's work and effort should be in the field of evangelism and missionary action. However, the story itself does not suggest the evangelistic or missionary task of the church. It is not a story of how a shepherd added another sheep to his flock. There are one hundred sheep at the beginning of the story and one hundred sheep at the end. There is no increase, no expansion, no growth of the flock.

If the shepherd had discovered a wild sheep in the wilderness, had gone out, captured it, and come back to the village with one hundred and one sheep, then the parable could conceivably be directed toward a missionary interpretation. Or if the shepherd had encountered a neglected sheep of one of his neighbor's flocks and proselyted it into his own flock, thereby returning with one hundred and one sheep, it might have evangelistic implications. But neither is the case. The shepherd leaves home with one hundred sheep and he returns with the same one hundred sheep.

The story of the Lost Sheep is actually about the **restoration** of a lost member of the flock, not an addition to it. Lang in his book *Pictures and Parables* observes that in all three of the "lost" parables the lost object or person was related to the seeker. The sheep was the property of the village, the coin the personal treasure of the woman, and the prodigal the beloved son in the father's house. "None of these features is true of an unregenerate sinner. The unbeliever is not one of the Lord's lost sheep."[11] Lang then concludes that these parables are not directed to the outsiders but to the **backsliders** — those who have once belonged, but have been separated from the fold and have now to be restored.

This was the presumed status of the sinners with whom Christ was associating. They were not heathen or Gentiles; they were citizens of the kingdom and children of God who had been relegated to second class citizenship. They had become separated from the mainstream of Israel because of their occupations or evil deeds. The Pharisees and Jewish religious leaders had classified them as undesirables and had "excommunicated" them from God's people.

Jesus made it clear that in the beginning of his ministry he considered his mission not as a great world outreach but as a ministry first to the Jews. In Matthew 15:24 when the Canaanite woman comes to him asking that her daughter be healed, Jesus says to her: "I have been sent only to the lost sheep of the people of Israel." Here Jesus' own word exegetes the parable of the Lost Sheep and defines and identifies who the lost sheep are. They are not the Gentiles, pagans, and unbelievers, but members of the people of Israel who have been separated and become lost.

Some translators use the word "outcast" for sinners. This is clearer and more to the point. They are outcasts **from** Israel. No place in the Gospels does the word "sinner" mean Gentile, pagan or unbeliever. It is always used as a class of Israelites who, for one reason or another, has been cut off, cast out, and thereby lost. Therefore, the parable of the Lost Sheep is not directed to the missionary task of recruiting unbelievers, but it is directed to the restoration of believers, children of God, bringing them back into full participation in the fellowship of believers.

Now there will be those who will be quick to point out that all men — pagans, heathen, unregenerate sinners and nonbelievers — are still children of God because he is their creator. Therefore, they are separated from God and do fall within the scope of the parable. This is perhaps true in the light of the total teachings of the New Testament. But honesty demands we recognize that this parable is concerned with restoration of lapsed members and not the recruiting of new ones. In the light of the new heremeneutics which presents the progressive meaning of a text it may be possible to use this parable as the basis of an evangelistic or missionary sermon. That may be its meaning now, but it was not its meaning then.

Shepherd

Parable begins, "What man of you . . ." according to the King James version, or "Suppose one of you . . ." according to the Good News version. It does not mention the word "shepherd." Now that is curious. The word "shepherd" had connotations in the minds of first century Jews, and one wonders if Jesus, when he told the story, and Luke, when he recorded it, purposely avoided the use of the term "shepherd" because of this.

As was mentioned above, shepherds as a group were classified as sinners because their long hours in the wilderness prevented them from regular attendance at the temple and synagogue. But on the other hand, "shepherd" as a symbol from the Old Testament was a revered figure. Moses was characterized as a shepherd of God's people who led them out of Egypt. In Exodus 3:1 his faithful tending of the sheep and his search for a lost lamb is what motivates God to say: "If Moses is so careful of his own sheep, how much more will he be of my people? I will make him a shepherd of Israel."

The good kings of Israel were referred to by Ezekiel as "shepherds" (Ezekiel 34). God himself is identified as a shepherd in the Twenty-third Psalm. How the rabbis and Pharisees managed to revere the shepherd-image of the Old Testament and at the same time call the real-life shepherds of their own day sinners is difficult to understand.This may be why Jesus avoided using the term "shepherd." He may have wanted to make it clear he was speaking about a contemporary flesh-and-blood shepherd, and was in no way appealing symbolically to the Old Testament image of shepherdhood.

Jesus looked directly at the Pharisees and teachers of the Law and said to them, "Suppose one of you . . ." Since his accusers looked on the keeping of sheep as a sinful occupation, this must have caused some raised eyebrows at the very beginning of his story. One can almost imagine a smile on our Lord's face as he spoke these words.

However, the important thing for the interpretation at this point of the story is that even though Jesus did not use the term "shepherd," this is what he meant. He wanted his listeners to imagine themselves as shepherds. Now it is not incidental that the shepherd-image is an **in-image.** A shepherd's job was not to create flocks but to protect and preserve them. Their primary task was not to enlarge the number in their charge but to maintain the flock intact. The shepherd-image is never used in the New Testament to symbolize one who recruits or evangelizes. He is not the one who goes out and "beats the bushes" to bring in new members; he is the pastor whose major responsibility is to care for and protect and give comfort to those who are already in the fellowship.

This is another reason for not using this text as a basis for evangelistic or missionary sermons. The vision of a shepherd going out with lantern in hand to knock on strange doors to get people to accept him as shepherd and join his flock is totally foreign to the New Testament. It is a product of twentieth-century churchmanship and romantic Sunday school art — it is not an idea presented in the New Testament.

Community Loss

Levison,[12] in his study of the background of the parables, points out that because of the strict ritualistic laws governing clean food, many pious Jews kept goats, sheep, and cows in order to make sure of having legally clean milk. The average family in the village would have about five to fifteen animals and they with their neighbors would put their animals together and hire a shepherd to tend them. The shepherd would get a monthly wage, and would be responsible for the welfare of the animals in his charge. If an animal died he must bring back the skin in such a condition that the owner can ascertain if the animal were willfully harmed or accidentally injured. If the shepherd could not prove he had not stolen and sold the animal he had to pay for it.[13]

Now this would indicate that the eagerness of the search for the lost sheep was not just a sentimental attachment the shepherd had for the sheep, but it was the result of the legal responsibility he had for its safety. The sheep belonged to the community and this is where the real concern was. This does not imply, however, that the shepherd was a "hireling." More than likely he was also a member of the village and some of the sheep were his own.

This does, however, explain the "joy" of his friends and neighbors when the lost sheep was found and brought home. More than likely the flock was returned to the village fold by another shepherd and word quickly got around that the village shepherd was still out in the wilderness searching for a sheep that had wandered off from the flock. In a poor village this was bad news and it traveled fast. If a man owned only a few sheep, the loss of one was a serious blow to him. So when the shepherd finally returned carrying on his shoulders the lost lamb, this would be a cause for great joy in the entire village.

Burden Of Restoration

When the shepherd finds the lost sheep he rejoices despite the fact that he is forced to carry the heavy sheep for a long distance. Remember that the sheep was lost in the wilderness which was a long way from the village and the farms that surrounded it. A lost sheep will lie down helplessly and refuse to move when separated from the other sheep. So the shepherd must pick it up, place it about his shoulders, and carry it home.

Therefore, finding the lost sheep is only a minor part of **restoring** a lost sheep. Carrying the lost home is really the hard work of restoration. It is what Bailey refers to as "the burden of restoration,"[14] and it is as important to the story as is the joy of finding. The whole community shares the joy, but the shepherd must assume the real burden of restoration. He must carry the lost sheep home.

Meaning

We have said that Jesus told this parable to vindicate his mission to the lost sheep of Israel. God wanted his chosen people to be one people. He wanted no second class citizens in his Kingdom. When some were cast out and treated as outsiders, God seriously felt their loss and went out and searched for them until they were found and returned to the flock.

Theologically this presented a radically new view of repentance. The lost did not repent in the judgment of the Pharisees. Yet Jesus says, "There is joy in heaven over one sinner who repents." In the light of the parable our Lord tells, this can mean only one thing — "being found," according to Christ, is equated with repentance. A sinner experiences repentance when he is found and restored. It is not something that the sinner must do, as the Pharisees had insisted, but it is something done to and for him! Repentance thereby becomes not a prerequisite of restoration but the result of it. Is is not an act of man but an activity of God for man.

Mutual Concern Of The Brethren

Now what does this parable say to us? Since the lost sheep is not an outsider brought in as a new member of the community, but a lost member of the community restored, it is not a parable about evangelistic or missionary endeavors but a parable about the mutual concern of the brethren.

It is about members of the church who get into trouble. If a member commits a crime, loses his job, gets hopelessly in debt, faces a divorce, loses a loved one, or becomes involved in a personal scandal, we should not ignore him but rush to his side.

If a member becomes indifferent or disinterested and drifts away from the church and becomes a backslider, he should become our major concern. Anything that would separate or alienate a member from the fellowship creates a situation of the lost sheep. The parable says that we are to drop everything and rush to his side. If he is out of work or in debt, help him financially. If he commits a crime, stand by him, visit him, and work for his release from prison, and welcome him back into the fellowship when he gets out. If he is sorrowing, comfort him. If he is lonely, visit him. If he is in trouble, help him. If he is disinterested, go to him and show concern for him and interest in him.

Not Easy

Now the parable points out that mutual consolation of the brethren and restoring them to full citizenship in the Kingdom is not going to be easy. Remember that it is not just finding of the lost sheep but the hard work of carrying the lost back to the community that is the "burden of restoration." It is never easy for a respectable fellowship to risk its reputation in a community by embracing undesirables. But the real test of the church is not its evangelistic programs, its growth in membership, or the amount of money it gives to world missions, as important as all these are; rather, the acid test of a church is the mutual consolation of its brethren.

If a church is a close, warm, caring, united fellowship, then evangelism and missionary efforts will flow as naturally from such a fellowship as a good tree produces a bumper crop of good fruit.

Nothing is really gained by adding new members to a fellowship of believers, if it is not a true and caring fellowship. Members are not added to the church as ornaments are hung on a Christmas tree — they are grafted as living branches and become one with the vine.

Congregation Of Shepherds

When we as baptized Christians within the church hear this parable we should not only identify ourselves with the lost sheep who have been found, but we should also identify with the shepherd whose task it is to find and search out the lost. As a congregation of the church we are the Body of Christ, and as such, a congregation of shepherds. Our task is not just to be grateful recipients of the shepherd's efforts, but at the same time be participants in the shepherd's efforts.

As Christ was the priest who offered the sacrifice and was at the same time the sacrificial lamb that was slain, so we are at the same time both the found sheep and the seeking shepherd. And here is the amazing truth of seeking — as we search for others we are assured and made more secure in our own found status.

During the Second World War in Northern France a group of soldiers was separated from its company during a severe snowstorm. As they wandered blindly in the blizzard, they came across the remains of a bombed-out farmhouse. It offered them partial shelter from the storm. But one of the young men was so concerned for others who might still be lost in the storm that he left his buddies huddled together in a corner of the ruins and went out to search for those who might yet be lost. All night long he circled the vicinity of the farmhouse calling out in the darkness hoping that lone stragglers might hear his voice and join him.

In the morning the storm was over and as the sun rose over the rolling hills, he saw his company coming down the road. He rushed back to the farmhouse to tell his companions they had been found, but to his horror he found them still huddled together frozen to death. The concern that drove him out to search for others was the very activity that kept him alive.

So as we search as shepherds we insure our "foundness" as sheep. As Christ says, "Losing your life, you find it." We are never so secure in our found-sheep status as when we are under-shepherds of the Great Shepherd and participate with him as he searches for the lost.

The parable of the Lost Sheep is a call from Christ to become shepherds in him, to be a loving, caring, sharing community in the world that the world seeing us might know that the Kingdom of God has truly come.

Broad Shoulders of Love

One more thing needs to be added. We have looked at the parable as Christ's refutation of the Little Bo Peep theology of the Pharisees toward the lost — "let them alone and they'll come home, wagging their tails behind them." In place of this our Lord testifies to the radical and agressive love of God that drives him forth boldly to search out and find the lost.

The parable, however, says more. It gives us a picture of God carrying the lost sheep home on his shoulders. And this is the gospel. He is not leading the sheep, or driving him home; he is carrying him. God willingly accepts not only the responsibility of finding lost sheep; he also finds joy in the burden of restoration. This presents to us not only a vision of the task of shepherdhood but the loving method used. For it is God's good pleasure not to return men to his Kingdom with a whip, as wild animals are driven, nor with a leash as dumb animals are led, but he desires to return lost people to his Kingdom carried on the broad shoulders of love. So he bore the cross. So he bears us up in love.

Notes

1. Joachim Jeremias, **Rediscovering the Parables,** (New York: Charles Scribner and Sons, 1966), p. 105.
2. Marcus Dods, **The Parables of Our Lord,** (New York: Fleming H. Revell), p. 331.
3. Edwin McNeill Poteat, **Parables of Crisis,** (New York: Harper and Brothers, 1950), p. 159.
4. Hugh Martin, **The Parables of the Gospels and Their Meaning for Today,** (London: SCM, 1937), p. 162.
5. Jeremias, op. cit., p. 106.
6. Dods, op. cit., p. 335.
7. W.O.E. Oesterley, **The Gospel Parables in the Light of Their Jewish Background,** (London: SPCK, 1936), p. 182.
8. N. Levison, **The Parables: Their Background and Local Setting,** (Edinburgh: T. & T. Clark, 1926), p. 146.
9. Eta Linnemann, **Jesus of the Parables,** (New York: Harper and Row, 1964), p. 71.
10. A.M. Harvey, **Companion to the New Testament,** (Oxford: Oxford University Press, 1971), p. 265.
11. G.H. Lang, **Pictures and Parables,** (London: Paternoster Press, 1955), p. 246.
12. Levison, op. cit., p. 151.
13. Ibid., p. 152.
14. Kenneth E. Bailey, **Poet and Peasant,** (Grand Rapids: Eerdmans, 1976), p. 153.

The
Swish
Of
A
Broom

5

THE PARABLE OF THE LOST COIN
Luke 15:8-10

One of life's most frustrating experiences is to misplace something around the house. You know that it has to be somewhere in the house but you just can't find it. This was the situation of the woman in the parable of the Lost Coin. Luke says that she has ten silver coins and loses one of them. Jeremias believes the story is talking about a coin from a woman's headdress. It was probably part of her dowry representing "her most precious possession, her nest egg, which may not be laid aside even in sleep."[1]

She suddenly discovers that this valuable coin is missing. Now it really wasn't lost in the sense that the sheep was lost. The shepherd might have had some idea where the lost sheep was. After all, a sheep could only wander off so far in the wilderness. But there was an urgency in his search because being separated from his protective care, the sheep might be set upon by wild animals and killed. He was confident that if he searched long enough, the animal would be found, but it might be too late and the sheep would be dead.

The woman faced no such urgency with her misplaced coin. As long as she had patience and continued searching she would eventually find it, and it would be no less valuable for having been lost.

The coin was also not lost in the sense that the prodigal was lost. The lost son had a mind of his own. He deliberately went away. And if he decided not to be found by his father, no amount of searching on the part of the father would have proved successful. Therefore, the appropriate response of the father toward his lost son was as Thielicke identifies him to be, "The Waiting Father." The coin, however, had no will or mind of its own. It just lay in its misplaced state and waited to be found.

Some writers have seen in the three stories of lostness three insights into how persons are lost from God. Land, for example, comments, "The sheep is lost by mere instinct of its silly, thoughtless nature; its wandering was more folly than crime. The coin was lost through no intent or carelessness of its own . . . no act of will. The son was lost by his selfish, perverted, intentional act and deed."[2] Chapel says the sheep was lost because he had no sense of direction.[3] The coin was lost because it was out of circulation and could render no service. The son was lost because he was squandering and wasting what his father had given him.

Some writers go so far as to see a progression in the three stories. The coin, an inanimate object, is lost. The sheep, an animal, is lost. And finally the son, a person, is lost. Now these speculative interpretations are interesting, but for our understanding of the parable of the Lost Coin the most important difference when compared with the other two parables is **where** it was lost.

The coin is lost in the house and this determines how the woman searches for the coin. She goes through three steps, each becoming progressively more intense. These steps show an ever-increasing determination on the part of the woman to locate her misplaced coin.

First, when she discovers that the coin is lost, she lights a lamp. Peasant houses in the days of our Lord had few if any windows. So she lighted a lamp. More than likely it was a simple wick in a saucer of oil giving very little light, but she did hope that it might provide enough light to at least give a glimmer of reflection if it happened to fall on the coin. This effort failed.

So, more determined, she took a broom and started to

sweep the house. Now the floor was either hard clay or rough stone and sweeping was not a certain promise of success. The coin could have lodged in a crevice or rough place in the floor and resisted the straws of the broom. But she listened, hoping to hear a tinkle of the coin on the floor if the broom hit it and knocked it loose. This, too, proved unsuccessful.

Still more determined than ever, she gets down on her hands and knees and examines every nook and cranny of her room until she finds it. Anyone who has ever lost a contact lens in a shag carpet will know the extreme persistence that is demanded to separate each strand and fiber of the rug until the lens is found. So the parable of the Lost Coin presents a progressively persistent search until the lost is found.

It might be said that first the woman used her eyes hoping to catch a glimmer of light from the coin. Then her ears, listening as she swept for a tinkle of the coin on the stone floor, and finally she used her fingers to examine by touch every inch of the room. She literally used her whole self and most of her physical senses to locate the lost coin.

Now the plot parallel to this story could be God's progressively persistent search for his people. God puts the full power of his personhood into the search to seek out and find his lost children. He searches for man as prophet, priest, and king and finally becomes flesh in his son in one last effort to save his rebelling children.

As we participate with God in his redemptive activity we, too, need to enter into the task with our whole personhood. To find the lost takes not only sharp eyes, alert ears, and willing hands, but the total dedication of our whole selves to the task. As one theologian-preacher has put it, being a Christian doesn't take much of a man but it takes all there is of him.

Belongingness

Now why did the woman so diligently and persistently search for her lost coin? If, as the text states, she had only ten coins and lost one of them, she was actually searching for ten per cent of her worldly possessions. That would seem to be sufficient reason for being stubbornly persistent. But so far as the dramatic logic of the story is concerned, the more obvious reason is that the coin **belonged to her**. If someone would have offered her a silver coin to give up the search, she would more than likely have refused. For as Jeremias points out, this coin was part of her dowry.[4] She had worn it on her person for years. She was attached to it because it was hers and a part of her life and no other coin could really take its place.

In the Midwest one sunny but cold afternoon, a little boy fell through the ice on the local pond. His friends rushed to the general store near by and there was a group of men just coming out of the back room of the store where a meeting had taken place. When the men heard what had happened, all started immediately toward the pond except one man. He said he had to stay and take care of the store. "After all," he said, "fourteen grown men ought to be able to save one little boy."

When the men got to the pond they saw that the ice was too thin to support the weight of a standing man. So they slid out onto the ice on their stomachs to distribute the weight of their bodies on the fragile ice. By so doing they could form a human chain out to the hole in the ice and rescue the drowning boy. But when they did, they were one man short and the boy slipped beneath the ice and was gone.

As the men came back up the hill to the store, they saw the man who said he wasn't needed, and they could hardly find the words to tell him that it was his own little boy.

If that father had known that it was his son who had fallen through the ice, nothing or no one could have stopped him. He would have been the first man to the pond. For, you see, belongingness makes a great deal of difference.

So the woman in our parable searched in a progressively persistent way because the coin belonged to her and had special meaning for her. How or why the woman lost the coin is not mentioned in the story. She may have dropped it accidentally, or misplaced it out of sheer carelessness, or even thrown it away in a fit of anger. However it happened is not important. The vital fact that motivated her actions is that the coin belonged to her, and even in its lost state it still belonged to her. And so God searches for the lost because they belong to him. They are not just lost sinners; they are his lost children. Even in their lost state they still belong to him.

This says something to us about our attitudes toward the large majority of people of our country who answer surveys that they believe in God but are not members of a church or ever attend a worship service. No amount of indifference or disinterest can destroy their "belongingness" to God.

And for that minority that will not even admit a belief in God there is still a mark of belongingness on their person. It is the shadow of the cross that falls across their lives and the words of God, "God so loved the **world** that he gave his only begotten son . . . ."

A careless teenager speeding down the street in his souped-up car lost control of it, jumped the curb, struck and killed a little girl. His car came to a stop as it crashed into a tree. The young man climbed from his car and seeing what he had done, ran for the hills. He found an abandoned mine and hid in it. When the sheriff arrived it was easy to trace the young driver, for he had left a trail of blood leading up to the opening of the mine.

When the sheriff and his men arrived at the mine they discovered that the young man was trapped just inside the opening by falling timber that had given way as he climbed into the mine. The opening left was too small for the sheriff or his men to enter, so a tall, thin man standing among the spectators volunteered to rescue the boy. He slid through the narrow opening and in a few moments emerged with the injured teenager.

A reporter who was on the scene recognized that the man who saved the boy was the father of the little girl that was killed. So he asked him how he could risk his life to save a kid who had just killed his child. The young father answered, "My first thoughts were to let him die. He deserves it. But then as I heard his pathetic cries for help all I could think of was — Christ died for him, too!"

That is the mark upon each person, no matter how far he pursues his lost state of rebellion from God. It is the mark of the cross which declares that each and every person belongs to God.

Until

One more thing needs to be said about this parable. It is that power-packed little phrase "until she finds it." The woman in the parable searches for her coin until she finds it. She doesn't give up. Progressively she intensifies her search. First the light of the lamp, then the swish of the broom, and finally the careful inch-by-inch examination of the whole house. So with God; he does not give up the search with the first refusal or failure. God persists.

The father of the prodigal persistently waited. Undoubtedly every time dust rose from the road indicating that someone was approaching, the father rushed out of the house to see if by chance it might happen to be his son returning home. The shepherd poked every bush with his crook and explored every crevice and ravine searching for his lost lamb, just as the woman threw her entire self into the search for the lost coin. And when we realize that our Lord told these stories to illustrate God's divine determination to search out and find those separated from him, when we hear such a gospel of God's good grace for us, certainly the joy in our hearts could only be matched by the joy in heaven, the joy of God over one sinner that repents. "Until he finds!" That is the gospel, the glorious good news that should penetrate into every dark corner of our world where the lost wait to be found. Listen! for there you will hear the swish of a broom.

Notes

1. Joachim Jeremias, **Rediscovering the Parables,** (New York: Scribner and Sons, 1966), p. 107.
2. G.H. Lang, **Pictures and Parables**, (London: Paternoster Press, 1955), p. 247.
3. Clovis Chapel, **Sermons from the Parables,** (New York: Abingdon-Cokesbury Press, 1933), pp. 167-179.
4. Jeremias, op. cit., p. 106.

124

The Honesty Of A Dishonest Man

6

THE PARABLE OF THE UNJUST STEWARD
Luke 16:1-13

Dr. Clark Kerr made a classic comment when he was dismissed as president of the University of California. He said, "I left the presidency as I entered it, fired with enthusiasm."[1] The parable of the Unjust Steward is the story of a man who was "fired with enthusiasm." As a story of a cleverly conceived crime, you would expect to find it in the morning newspaper under bold headlines, rather than on the lips of our Lord. It talks about embezzlement, fraud, altered ledgers, and a rogue who cheats his master even after he has been fired. But the most shocking aspect of the story is that Jesus apparently praised this dishonest rogue and held him up as an example for us all.

It is undoubtedly one of the most baffling of the parables. Interpreters are perplexed and confused as to whether the steward should wear a white hat or a black one. On the one hand he is called resourceful, practical, prudent, shrewd and clever, a man of foresight, ingenuity and gumption. On the other hand he is charged with being unjust, unrighteous, dishonest, unscrupulous and defrauding. He is called a grafter, a rogue, a rascal, and a crook. The difficulty in knowing whether to put a black or a white hat on him is due to the fact that he is a man who does a bad thing well. He is a clever crook. You can compliment or condemn him according to how you look at him.

The ancient and medieval church tried to interpret the parable allegorically. Theophilus of Antioch thought the steward was Paul who squandered God's possessions by persecuting the church. He was then confronted by

Christ to give an account of his misguided stewardship and as a result replaced the hardness of the Law with the goodness of the gospel message. Others of this period have seen in the figure of the steward Judas the betrayer and even Satan himself.

Critics outside the church used this parable as an example and proof of the fact that Jesus was only a fallible man and told stories that were not even morally valid. Critics within the church have challenged the right of this parable to be included in the canon of the New Testament.

This difficulty in understanding the parable was apparently the case even earlier in the history of its use, for appended to it are what appear to be interpretations or applications of the parable. They are frequently called logions. C.H. Dodd believes they are "preacher's notes." He comments, "We can almost see here notes for three separate sermons on the text."[2] C.W.F. Smith thinks that they are obviously "variant interpretations from different expositors"[3] already attached to the story by the time Luke first heard it in the oral tradition and decided to record it in his writings.

These three notations or logions each presents its own focal point of interest within the parable. The first deals with the importance of decisive action in a crisis. The second deals with the wise use of money, and the third deals with faithfulness. Considered one at a time, they can serve to organize the various interpretations scholars have given to the parable. This we will do in the discussion which follows.

The first logion — "the people of this world are much more shrewd in handling their affairs than the people who belong to the light" — is the most common interpretation of the parable. It is the lesson that decisive, bold action is demanded in a crisis. For Hunter the coming of Jesus bringing both blessing and judgment was a crisis hour for Israel. Jesus saw that his people were in a similar situation to the dismissed steward, except that the crisis which they faced was far more terrible. Therefore the Jews should size up their situation shrewdly and act boldly.[4]

Francis Filas believes the parable was intended to shame good people "who have an eternally worthwhile cause but do not work for it."[5] Glen sees this steward as a "realist." He states, "Here was a man in a critical situation who did something about it."[6] The parable thereby becomes an appeal for decisive faith. Glen sees the parable as directed to the unconverted, the indifferent, the doubtful and the hesitant. "For although the world is what it is, with its daily record of scandal, there is often an amazing manifestation of shrewd maneuvering, of studied devices for gaining advantages in questionable areas of business and politics, and quite often of quick discernment of a threat to material security. But the tragedy is that the same sagacity is not exhibited toward the real predicament."[7] This real predicament is the age-old question, "Who am I?" and a second question equal in importance to the first, "What is the meaning of life?" These are the crisis questions Christ creates in our minds as he comes and confronts us with his Kingdom.

For Jeremias this is a parable about impending judgment. Jesus is speaking to the people facing "the hour of decision," and a quick and resolute action must be taken. Jeremias places this parable in a section entitled "The Challenge of the Hour." He believes that Jesus is saying to us that we are soon to stand before the judge. Therefore, "clear the matter up while there is still time. Acknowledge your debts. Ask your opponent for indulgence and patience. If you do not succeed in doing so, the consequences will be terrible."[8]

Granskou agrees with Jeremias and adds, "To act quickly in the face of certain situations in history and life is the highest sign of prudence."[9] According to Granskou this means that the preacher needs not only to understand this parable, but to be well-versed in the

130

issues and problems of our day that bring impending crisis into people's lives.

All of these interpretations in one way or another see this parable as a story about the honesty of a basically dishonest man. Though he was dishonest in most of his daily dealings, charging exorbitant interests, cheating everyone he could, he was nevertheless at one point in his life very honest. He was honest about himself and the crisis situation in which he stood. He suddenly realized that what he cherished so dearly, worked for so diligently could be taken away from him in an instant. The boss spoke two words, "You're fired," and he lost his job, his income, and with it his future security.

Christ says that his coming is a crisis hour. It calls everything we value most into question. It literally turns our lives upside-down. Instead of striving to get, now we will learn to serve. Instead of being masters, we will become servants. Instead of working our way upward to heaven, the Lord of heaven will come down to us.

Now it is a great distance from the first to the twentieth century. For most of us the legs of our imagination will not stretch that far. It is just too big a step. Besides, we are not accustomed to associating Christ with crisis. He is the answer, not the problem. He brings peace, not confusion and turmoil. So when a parable comes implying that Christ's coming brings crisis we are ill-prepared for it. We know about the energy crisis, the economic crisis, and the crisis of a terminal disease, but only radical store-front evangelists treat Christ as a crisis. Perhaps we have lived so long apart from the truth that we have become calloused and indifferent. We find it easy to be dishonest with ourselves, so long as we are successful. So we accept dishonesty as normal. This does not mean that we cheat, or lie, or steal in our business and social lives, but rather we constantly cheat ourselves, and lie to ourselves about what is really important in life. We bury our heads in the sands of sophistication.

Sin becomes an old-fashioned out-of-date conception. Value is limited to a good bargain at the local store. We never really come to grips with the meaning of our lives. We fill up the emptiness and loneliness of our days with television and shabby entertainment. We hide the ugliness of ourselves with cosmetics and expensive clothes. We wear diamonds and mink to direct attention away from what we are to what we possess. We are prosperous prodigals who have run away from home and have become successful. Therefore, we feel no need to run home to the father's house and no need for him to run out and embrace us. We tear down the pig sties and build in their places skyscrapers of steel and glass. We lay streets of concrete over the mud and filth that forms the foundations of our little worlds and call it progress.

And when Christ comes to us as he does in this parable, pointing out the importance of facing the real crisis of our lives and acting decisively, we don't know what he is talking about. When he presents us with the story of a dishonest man, and says that this man is better off — wiser — than you because he honestly faced the fact that he is in trouble and his future is in danger, we are shocked. But the truth is, the plot of the parable speaks directly to us, pointing out that profits and progress do not guarantee future security. One day our skyscrapers will fall, our cosmetics will fade, our fancy clothes will wear out, our concrete highways will crumble away, dumping us back into the mudhole we have built our progress on. Our Lord says to us in this parable that before this happens we should wake up, and face up to the crisis of his coming. All that we value so much is meaningless. Therefore, turn to true treasures.

Wise Use of Wealth

The second logion added to the parable is, "Make friends for yourselves with worldly wealth, so that when it gives out you will be welcomed into the eternal home." This is an appeal to the wise use of worldly wealth. This clearly refers to the parable and reflects Luke's placement of the parable in his total gospel. We see that immediately following the parable of the Unjust Steward Luke says (verse 14), "The Pharisees heard all this, and they made fun of Jesus because they loved money." Luke then follows this statement with the parable of the Rich Man and Lazarus, which would indicate that in this section of his writing Luke has brought together several teachings of Jesus concerning money.

In the story of the parable, the steward made friends out of foes by reducing their heavy debts. As Christians we are to do the same. We are to use our money to win friends and influence people, but instead of procuring for ourselves hospitable homes on earth we are to obtain an eternal home in heaven.[10] This creates difficulties. Just how is worldly wealth to be used to attain a heavenly home? The only possible solution to this question seems to be that given by Derrett who suggests that when the steward cut the debts owed his master, he was not cheating his own master but was cutting down or eliminating entirely his own usurious profits.[11]

At the time Jesus told this parable, graft was a common practice among stewards and people in charge of managing estates. If a man came and wanted to borrow forty barrels of olive oil, the steward would figure the master should get ten barrels of oil as a fair interest on the loan. This would mean that the borrower would owe fifty barrels to the master. Then the steward would add a usurious profit for himself of fifty barrels, making the total debt owed one hundred barrels of oil. When the debt was finally settled, the master would get his ten per cent, but the steward would get a nifty profit of fifty barrels of oil for himself.

This may seem like an unbelievable economic condition, but it is characteristic of the profession of the middle man to make greater profits than the worker or the producer. The classic example of this is the story of the enterprising fellow who set up a booth in the market place. He had a front and a rear window in his booth. A farmer came to the front window with two pigs. He needed a new suit. A tailor came to the rear window with suits. He was looking for a pig. So the middle man took the two suits and the two pigs. He traded two suits for one pig and two pigs for one suit. The farmer went home happy with his new suit. The tailor was more than satisfied to get a pig for his dinner. And the middle man ended up with twice as much as either of the other two men. He did nothing but manage the exchange and he got a pig and a new suit for his service.

So the steward in our story had the power to make as much profit as he could get away with. The profit may sound unreasonable and it may have been exaggerated to increase the dramatic impact of the story, but it is really not out of line with what we know historically of the profits of middlemen. Arthur Voobus, studying the evidence of ancient papyri, the writings of Josephus, and the records of rabbis, finds that exorbitant profit was the common practice.[12] The owners of estates lived in the hills enjoying the cool weather and complete relaxation, free from all the sweaty activities and worries of everyday business. They were content to let their steward manage the estate any way he wanted, so long as a fixed income came to them as masters and owners.

This being the case, what we have in our parable is a story of a steward who was getting rich charging exorbitant rates of interest. When he was faced with the crisis of being fired, he decided to change his ways and begin helping the people he had for so long a time wronged. So he cut the debts of the people by eliminating his own profit. What he gave to the debtors came out of his own pocket. He was not committing a fraud or cheating his master in any way. The master would still get what was rightfully his. He was not feathering his nest by plucking his master's profits.

This is the reason the steward was praised. He had turned over a new leaf. He was attempting to set straight his wrongdoings and evil ways. His relationship to the tenants was now diametrically opposite to what it had been. Instead of loading them down with huge interest rates, he was easing their burdens. And in this way he hoped to win their gratitude and friendship.

His actions are clear. At a moment of crisis in his life he had learned a great lesson — people are not to be exploited but served — **people** are more important than **profits**. The steward established a new relationship with his fellowmen. When the parable is seen in this light, the lesson it teaches is consistent to one of the basic teachings of our Lord. Namely, relationship to our fellowmen is the fundamental requirement for true righteousness. When the young lawyer came to Christ asking him, "What must I do to inherit eternal life?", Jesus combined love for God with love for all persons as the great commandment of God's will. To love and serve one another is "like unto" loving and serving God. At the Last Judgment Christ presents service to the needy as the test of one's eternal destiny. Here in this parable our Lord is saying the same thing. This steward is to be praised for he has changed from exploiting people to serving them. He has turned foes into friends. Voobus comments, "This is the only security because it is the only atmosphere which nourishes the life of faith and makes it real."[13]

The steward had learned a lesson all of us need. He learned that money is an excellent servant but a treacherous master. And he also learned the even greater lesson that people are more important than profits. Dr. John Rilling in *Insights* puts it this way: "Our problem, yours and mine, is not to end up, as one man put it, as his ambition 'to be the richest man in the cemetery,' but to

use our time, talents and money to make life easier for
our fellows, to lift the crushing burden of poverty. We
can't buy our way into heaven, but we can try to make
this life a little more like heaven."[14]

Faithfulness

The third logion concerns faithfulness. "Whoever is
faithful in small matters will be faithful in large ones;
whoever is dishonest in small matters will be dishonest
in large ones. If then you have not been faithful in
handling worldly wealth, how can you be trusted with
true wealth? And if you have not been faithful in what
belongs to someone else, who will give you what belongs
to you?"

Cadoux,[15] searching to discover who Jesus had in
mind when he told this parable, came to the conclusion
that there was only one set of people in the time of Jesus
who had dishonestly used that which had been entrusted
to them, and that was the high priests. They held their
office by appointment from Rome and it was common
knowledge that they had bartered the national ideal and
the interests of a spiritual trust in order to get Roman
favor and secure themselves in office. In John 19:15 it is
the high priests who shout, "We have no king but
Caesar." Cadoux sees Jesus doing the same thing with
this parable as he did physically when he drove the
money changers out of the temple. He is saying that the
high priests have abused the Court of the Gentiles by
making it a den of thieves when it should be a house of
prayer. "If they have been dishonest and unfaithful in
their use of what God intended to be a place where the
Gentiles might worship him, what of God can they claim
to have in themselves?"[16]

William Taylor believes that the parable of the
Unjust Steward is related to the parable of the Prodigal
Son which precedes it, and is therefore directed to the

Pharisees attempting to point out their unfaithfulness. There are other ways of misusing the portion God has given us than by riotous living. "One who appropriates as his own that which he has received in behalf of another is as really unfaithful to God as is the dissolute man who spends his substance on the gratification of appetite."[17]

Marcus Dod takes still another position and states that the parable was directed to the publicans. The Romans auctioned off the office of tax collecting. The first class of tax collectors was called "farmers" and they had subcontractors called "publicans." These were rich, monied men. They were known to be good executives, clever, hard-working and intelligent. Jesus directed this parable to the publicans, urging them to carry over into the Kingdom of God the same qualities that had made them successful in the world of business and commerce.

Wallace tells the story of Nathan Meyer Rothschild, member of the famous banking family which at one time ruled the finances of all Europe. Rothschild was at the battle of Waterloo as a spectator. At sunset, when he saw the French beginning to give way, he sprang into the saddle and rode all night, reaching the shore of the Channel at daybreak. He bribed a fisherman to take him across and he reached London thirty-six hours before anyone heard the news of Wellington's victory over Napoleon. He used those hours trading on the stock exchange to such advantage that he made nearly eight million dollars in one day.[18]

Now it was this kind of faithfulness and dedication in the realm of business by the children of darkness which Jesus admired and wanted to see as a characteristic of those who followed him.

Most scholars agree that Jesus is pictured in this logion as calling Christians to be as faithful and hard-working within the church as worldly men are in their affairs within the world. The problem is that this sounds very much like justification by the good works of faithfulness and accomplished deeds. Brunner meets this challenge head-on, asserting that we are saved by mercy and grace alone. We cannot make ourselves children of the light by any merit or effort of our own. We are children of the light because God lifts us out of darkness and places us in the light. "As a rescue party, searching in the mountains for victims who have fallen into an abyss, reaches down to the completely exhausted people, carrying them back to the light of day, and bringing them safely home with infinite care, thus God in Christ has sent his rescue party to our salvation and brought us to his shelter called the church, the community of Jesus Christ."[19] But now, adds Brunner, "we must return to work." There are new responsibilities in this state of "light." We are to be good stewards of the gifts and the blessings God has so freely given to us. We are to enter into competition with those who still dwell in darkness. We are to work just as hard, if not more so, than those who labor in the world, not to gain a reward but because we have been given a reward. As Paul puts it, we who have been given a crown of victory must run just as hard in the race as those who are striving to win a crown.

The new life gives us both small and great gifts and blessings. According to the parable we are to be equally faithful with both. Money, for example, may be a little blessing in our life. We may not have much of it, but we are to use what we have as faithful stewards of God and remember the widow's mite.

So the three logions — decisive action in crisis, wise use of wealth, and faithfulness — all present us with interesting insights into possible interpretations of this very difficult parable. But it is also possible to deal with the parable in and of itself — as a story apart from its setting and the attached logions.

This we will do from two different points of view. First, we will look at the parable assuming that the master was as dishonest as was his steward. It thereby

becomes a story of what happens when crooks fall out
with each other in their cleverly conceived schemes to
cheat common persons in need of money. Secondly, we
will look at the parable as the story of a master who was
merciful and how his steward used that mercy to his own
advantage.

The Crooked Master

Even though the steward is the main actor in the
story, the character of the master determines to a large
extent the interpretation of the parable. If he is seen as a
scheming business man who wants to make as much
money as possible and doesn't care how he does it, the
parable becomes an appeal to reform the social conditions of the day where people are exploited by racketeers.

In the days of our Lord there were crooked business
men who fleeced the public and kept the poor man in his
poverty with no possible means of escape. One of the pro-
tections the people had was the biblical laws against
usury — the lending of money at high rates of interest.
However, clever and crooked men could get around these
laws.

Say, for example, a man came to a wealthy businessman wanting to borrow one hundred dollars. The master
would say, "O.K. I'll loan it to you on this condition. One
hundred dollars is equal to ten bags of wheat. You write
down on this piece of paper that you owe me twenty bags
of wheat and it's a deal." The crime of usury would be
committed as the man borrows one hundred dollars and
has to pay the outrageous interest of one hundred per
cent. But there would be no evidence of such a monetary
transaction because the written record only indicated
that the man owed the master twenty bags of wheat.

Now this was a common practice in the first century
and the master in our parable could easily have been
such a man. And if he were, then our story is about a

crooked steward and his crooked master who were operating a village swindle as good as any of our modern racketeers could devise. Both the master and the steward would be hated citizens of the community and this would explain why the steward had to make friends fast when he was fired, because he had none. He was known in the village as a henchman and partner in crime with the crooked master. They were the local Mafia and instead of running a protection racket like the ones in New York and Chicago today, they had a loan racket and the people suffered and paid.

Then one day the master discovers that his steward is falsifying the accounts and taking a big cut off the top before ever turning over the receipts to the master. The bossman is furious and in great anger fires the steward on the spot. The steward panics. He must make friends fast and show the people in the village that he has been on their side all along but has been unable to do anything about it, for he fears the master as much as they do. But now things have gone too far and he is finally going to get out of this nasty job. He is going to betray the master and befriend the exploited debtors. So he sneaks into the master's office and gets the record of the loans. Speed is important because he must get the records changed before the master finds out they are missing.

The change must be in the borrower's handwriting, so the steward calls together all the debtors and gets them to change the notes and reduces the amount owed. When this is finished, the steward returns the altered accounts to the office.

The master is trapped. He realizes the next day that the records have been changed, but he can't do anything about it. The steward has been in on the swindle from the very beginning. To expose the steward would be to expose himself and his whole crooked usury business. The steward has played on the master's defect — his fraudulent business practices. He has beat the master at his own game. He has out-fleeced the master fleecer. What can the master do but laugh it off and say, "You are a damn clever fellow." The steward has tricked the master into being honest.

When the people first heard this story, they must have clapped their hands for sheer joy and some rolled on the ground holding their stomachs in uproarious laughter. How they hated these master crooks who charged usurious interests! Then to hear how one of them was cheated by his own kind and tricked into being honest was a great delight to hear.

Now if this were the real meaning of the story, what point would our Lord have been making? He certainly did not tell it simply as an entertaining tale of revenge. Rather, he must have wanted the people to see how this rogue dealt with the deceit and dishonesty of this master racketeer who had for so long taken advantage of the poor and oppressed people. After having told the story, he turned to the Jewish leaders with the challenging question of what they — the good people of the community — were doing about the racketeers who rob the elderly of their savings and loan money out at choking interests.

Those words must have fallen heavily upon his listeners as they do upon us two thousand years later. For crooked businessmen and racketeers still exploit little people who cannot defend themselves. And what do we do about it? As long as we are not directly involved, we do nothing! The corruption within labor unions, the bottomless greed of capital, the profit monsters that continuously push prices upward so that the poor face greater poverty and the average man lives on continuous credit hoping that next month might be better so he can pay up his past due bills. But we ignore it all and go along with a system we basically know is wrong. We close our eyes — not to pray but to evade our social responsibilities.

There is little doubt that this is an interesting

interpretation. If it is not what our Lord intended when he first talked about the clever steward, at least he more than likely would agree that the point made is extremely valid. For the people our Lord loved and associated with are today the victim's of crooked men both in business and politics.

The Merciful Master

We have seen what the parable might have meant if the master in the story was a crooked businessman; now let us see what happens to the story if we assume the master was a man of mercy. This is the interpretation which Kenneth E. Bailey presents in detail in his book *Poet and Peasant.*[20] This interpretation sees the parable as a series of dramatic acts, each one stressing the importance of mercy.

The first act begins with a steward being called into the presence of his master. He is accused of carelessness and neglect of duty. He is not accused of stealing or even being dishonest; he has simply wasted his master's funds. The Greek word used here is the same word that occurs in the parable of the prodigal son. Apparently the steward had enemies and they had told the owner the damaging truth about his employee. Since there are witnesses ready to testify, the steward makes no effort at defense. He admits the charges against him in the most obvious manner — he says nothing.

The impact of the disclosure upon the steward is a heavy blow. He panics. He had no illusions about future. The consequences of his conduct collide with his conscience and he knows that he is in a desperate situation. He cannot dig for a living; he is too weak. He cannot beg; he is too proud. The forecast of his future is bleak.

But what is often overlooked is that the master's treatment of him is mild and merciful. The law permits, and custom demands, that he either be thrown in jail or severely punished, such as by public whipping. If this were a Roman setting, he could actually be killed for such a dereliction of duty.

The master, however, does not exercise this right; rather he shows mercy. He doesn't even scold him; he simply fires him. Therefore, the dramatic impact of this first act is a picture of a guilty man who experiences the unusual and surprising mercy of his master.

In the second act we see the steward wrestling with his problem. He is thrown out of his job. He is not a man of muscle so he cannot dig. He is proud and cannot beg, but he is a man of ingenuity. He must now depend on the only thing left to him — his wits. Somehow he must work out a plan for his own salvation. He must not end up just another statistic on the unemployment rolls, because in this day before unemployment insurance no one is going to take care of him but himself. Besides, his job has not made him very popular with the people and this is an image he must drastically change. Somehow he must become the friend of working men rather than their foe and exploiter. Then he remembers his master's mercy toward him and suddenly a plan comes to him. The Greek word Luke uses here literally means "I got it!" He will utilize the unusual merciful nature of his master. The plan is born. He will risk everything on the fact that his master is a kind man. The key to his plan is that no one yet knows that he has been fired. Time is on his side, but he must act quickly.

Act three moves with great haste. Each debtor is called in and in his own handwriting is required to reduce the debt owed the master. The debtors are surprised at what is happening, but they have no way of knowing that deception is involved in this action. They assume that the dishonest steward is still the legitimate representative of the master. After all, the steward asks, "How much do you owe **my** master?" (verse 5b)

Now it is certain that the dishonest steward took full

advantage of this situation and tried to make them feel comfortable about what was happening. He made every effort to convince each debtor that he was the one who influenced the master to express this action of great generosity and unusual mercy. Bailey suggests that we can easily construct the kind of small talk that could have taken place during the bill changing:[21] "You know, of course, that I talked the old gentleman into this because I know how tough things have been for you this year." Well, everything worked out exactly as the dishonest steward had planned it.

The last act sees the dishonest steward gathering up all the changed accounts and delivering them to the master. Now the master takes one look at the changed bills and reflects on his alternatives. He knows that already the whole village is celebrating. They are praising him as a noble, generous, merciful master. He is greatly pleased as he hears the voices drifting up from the village singing, "For he's a jolly good fellow, which nobody can deny."

The master has two alternatives. He can go to his debtors and say that it was all a mistake. The steward was not his employee when the transaction occurred and therefore the actions are null and void. But if he does that now, the joy in the village will turn into instant anger and he will be cursed as a stingy tyrant. The master is truly a merciful man and he does not want to have the reputation of being a cruel and unkind person.

His second alternative is to keep silent and accept the praise of the village and allow the clever steward to ride high on his wave of popular enthusiasm. This would mean that the master would pay out of his own pocket the price of the dishonest steward's instant popularity. This way the master could save face in the situation and the steward would benefit once more from the master's great generosity and mercy.

The key word in each act of this drama is **mercy** —

the unusual and surprising mercy of the master. The steward experienced the mercy of the master when he was only fired and not flogged or jailed. The steward then created a situation in which his master showed generous mercy toward all his debtors. He risked everything on the fact that when his master found out, he would not do anything that would make him appear unmerciful before his fellowmen because the master **is** a merciful man.

The lesson drawn from this interpretation is obvious. God is a God of judgment but also of mercy. Therefore, when we confront the crisis of the Kingdom we have only one option and that is to entrust everything to the unfailing, surprising, unusual mercy of God. Because God is merciful, he will pay the price of our salvation out of his own pocket. We are to place our total trust on the mercy of God. Even though we are dishonest and disobedient wasters of God's good gifts, we can be saved as we place our trust in the unending mercy of God. So a difficult parable suddenly opens up and presents some fresh and exciting preaching possibilities.

Summary

The parable interpretations of the Unjust Steward begin with a note of the crisis facing man as the Kingdom comes in Christ, and end on a note of mercy. The harmonious theme that runs through these interpretations is pictorially presented in the story of the man shipwrecked on a desert island. For several months he managed to survive, hoping each day to be rescued. But as the months continued to pass, he accepted the fact that he may be on this island for many months, even years. So he began to accept his status and attempted to make the best of it. He built a little house, domesticated animals, planted crops. After the first year's crop, he built barns and storage shelters. In fact, he created a rather comfortable life for himself carved out of the wilderness by his own sheer toil. Then one day while he was out hunting, he noticed smoke rising from the direction of his farm home. He rushed back to the clearing only to see everything he had worked so hard to build in flames. Years of sweat and aching muscles all going up in flames. For him it was a crisis almost as great as the shipwreck that had brought him to this forsaken island. He was defeated. There was no more fight left in him — only frustration and fear. Then suddenly he heard voices. Could it be? He looked up and through his tear-smudged eyes he saw men running up the coast to rescue him. The smoke from his burning farm had been seen by a passing ship. What seemed to him to be a tragic crisis was at the same time the cause and opportunity for his salvation.

So for us. The coming of Christ and the resulting crisis in our lives can be for us our great opportunity. As the steward reacted boldly and decisively so must we. For we, like the steward, know that our master is merciful. To the world a young man dying on a cross is a stumbling block. It is a sign of weakness and defeat, but to us who are being saved it is the sign of power and victory. We boldly take the leap into darkness and trust that his arms of mercy will catch us and bear us up into the light.

Notes

1. **Insights,** Vol. I, Number 21, 18th Sunday after Pentecost.
2. Charles Dodd, **The Parables of the Kingdom,** (London: Nisbet and Co., rev. ed., 1961), p. 128.
3. Charles W. F. Smith, **The Jesus of the Parables,** (Philadelphia: United Church Press, 1975), p. 146.
4. Archibald M. Hunter, **The Parables Then and Now,** (Philadelphia: Westminster Press, 1971), p. 100.
5. Francis L. Filas, **The Parables of Jesus**, (New York: Macmillan, 1959), p. 76.
6. J. Stanley Glen, **The Parables of Conflict in Luke,** (Philadelphia: Westminster Press, 1962), p. 91.
7. Ibid., p. 93.
8. Joachim Jeremias, **Rediscovering the Parables,** (New York: Charles Scribner's Sons, 1966), p. 143.
9. David M. Granskou, **Preaching on the Parables,** (Philadelphia: Fortress Press, 1972), p. 99.

146

10. A. E. Harvey, **Companion to the New Testament,** (Oxford: Oxford University Press, 1971), p. 269.
11. J. Duncan Derrett, **Mosaic Law in the New Testament,** (London: Darton, Longman and Todd, 1970), pp. 48-77.
12. Arthur Voobus, **The Gospels in Study and Preaching,** (Philadelphia: Fortress Press, 1966), p. 275.
13. Ibid., p. 227.
14. **Insights,** Vol. I, Number 21, 18th Sunday after Pentecost.
15. A. T. Cadoux, **The Parables of Jesus,** (New York: Macmillan, 1931), p. 135.
16. Ibid., p. 137.
17. William Taylor, **The Parables of Our Savior,** (New York: A. C. Armstrong and Son, 1886), p. 372.
18. Ronald S. Wallace, **Many Things in Parables,** (New York: Harper and Brothers, 1955), p. 76.
19. Emil Brunner, **Sowing and Reaping,** (Richmond, Va.: John Knox Press, 1946,), pp. 80-81.
20. Kenneth E. Bailey, **Poet and Peasant,** (Grand Rapids: Eerdmans, 1976).
21. Ibid., p. 100.

That
Is
Not
Enough

7

THE PARABLE OF DIVES AND LAZARUS
Luke 16:19-31

Most of us have at one time or another dreamed of being rich. And I suppose that the rich have nightmares about becoming suddenly poor. This plot of reversal from poor to rich, rich to poor, has served as the basis for many a novel, play and short story. And it is the dramatic pattern from which our parable of Dives and Lazarus is woven. Sometimes it is considered one story with two acts. Other interpreters consider it to be two stories brought together by our Lord to present one single thought.

The first story is about the reversal of human destiny after death. The rich man is stripped of his privileged status and finds himself in Hades. The poor man ends up in the desirable bosom of Abraham. And the finality of this reversal is firmly established.

In the second story we hear Abraham refusing to give to Dives a special sign. He has Moses and the prophets and that is all he needs.

Act One

Act one is a well-known and commonly told story. It was originally an Egyptian folk tale dated about 331 B.C. It concerned the journey of Si-Osiris, the son of Setme Chamais, into the underworld which concludes with the words, "He who has been good on earth, will be blessed in the Kingdom of the Dead." The Alexandrian Jews brought this story back to Palestine where it became the story of the poor scholar and the rich publican Bar Majan.

By the time of Jesus it had become the story of a poor man named Lazarus, a rich man, and what happened to each of them after death. There are two possible ways to interpret the drama of this first act. First, attention could be placed on the fact that one man was rich and the other man was poor. In the afterlife their positions were reversed. The poor is privileged and the rich man is in need. Second, attention could be placed on the way the rich man treated the poor man so that the conclusion would be that such actions of indifference to human need will be punished and the good who suffer now will be rewarded in the after life.

However, the story itself would suggest not a moral interpretation as much as a social one. For the stress of detail is placed not on the badness of Dives but on the fact that he was very rich. The detail of the purple garment he wore, Voobus points out, was associated with royalty, and linen, which was mentioned, as the most prized fabric of antiquity; both were regarded by the people of the time as marks of extreme luxury.[1] Dives is the Latin name for a very rich man. So the details of the story — expensive clothes and the fact that he "lived in luxury every day" — would support the social contrast between these two men. On the other hand, there are no details which point out that Dives did anything bad at all to Lazarus. If he did anything wrong, the story would simply suggest that he ignored him.

The poor man is called Lazarus which means "God is my helper." Actually Lazarus is a nickname for "Eleazer" and would be used as we use the names Joe, Bill or Pete. This would imply that in contrast to Dives, Lazarus was a very ordinary type of guy. No dignity or status is given to him by the story. He is just a poor beggar at a rich man's gate.

The parable does mention that he is brought to the gate, which implies that he was either blind or crippled. His condition is described as "full of sores," more than likely running ulcers of the skin, because the dogs are pictured as licking the liquid from the open sores. Some writers have pointed out that the tongue of a dog was thought by primitive people to purify wounds and assist them to heal. However, the Greek word used here implies "an aggravation of the sick person's suffering."[2]

Here at the gate of Dives' great house Lazarus would eat the bread "that fell from the rich man's table." In affluent America this seems a most undesirable situation. We picture a starving man rummaging through garbage cans to find rotting morsels of food to save himself from starvation.

This, however, is unfair to the story and is greatly overdrawn in sermons on this text. The bread that Lazarus fed on was rather good eating and very nourishing. The parable even states that Lazarus hoped to "fill himself" with this bread. In the days of our Lord, bread was used as napkins. When dining, a person would tear off a piece of rich, juicy lamb and eat it. Then the fingers would be wiped with a piece of bread. As a result, this bit of bread would be soaked with gravy and the fat of meat and at times would contain generous chunks of meat itself. This bread was then discarded and gathered up by the servants. Although it lacked the gourmet appearance of the food that graced the rich man's table, it was mighty tasty and as nourishing as anything the rich man ate.

Bread was also used in place of spoons and forks. The bread would be dipped in gravies and sauces. The rule of etiquette at the time was that once such bread was dipped into the dish of gravy it could not be dipped again. So it had to be thrown away. This left-over bread used as forks and napkins was gathered by the servants and then taken out and given to the poor who waited patiently at the gate of the house.

It was this bread that Lazarus fed on and was commonly called "The Feast of Beggars." It should be

noted that if the story desired to stress that Dives was a
bad man, it would have presented him as refusing the
beggars and the poor at the gate and feeding the left-over
bread to his dogs. But it does not. Which gives added
support to the fact that what the parable wishes to point
out is that Dives was a very rich man and not a very
immoral man.

Dual Death

Both men die. Lazarus dies first and according to the
King James version is "carried by angels into Abraham's
bosom." This is a rarely used term and is understood as a
reference to the heavenly banquet. Lazarus is placed by
the angels at the side of Abraham reclining on his bosom,
according to the Good News version. Voobus, however,
appealing to the evidence of rabbinical writings, states,
"It becomes clear that contemporary thought regarded
Abraham as a custodian of the underworld. He has the
task of rescuing those loyal to the covenant (of Gen. 17).
Thus the phrase 'to be in Abraham's bosom' meant
simply 'to be circumcised and to have Abraham's
protection.' "[3]

The rich man also died and was buried, but he ended
up in Hades suffering great pain. Now the Jewish view of
the afterlife at the time of Jesus was not a uniform
doctrine. The Sadducees did not believe in a resurrection
of the dead and because of this some scholars like A. M.
Hunter, C. W. F. Smith and T. W. Manson, conclude that
the parable was directed against the Sadducean doctrine
that there is no life beyond the grave. The story plot of
the parable is not really designed to fit this purpose.[4]

Hades in the New Testament is a translation of the
Hebrew word "Sheol" used in the Septuagint and refers
to the place which receives all men at death, and where
they wait for the final judgment. Therefore, Hades is not
the same as our word "hell." The final state of torment in

the New Testament is Gehenna. It is true that Hades eventually developed into a place of punishment and became synonymous with Gehenna and hell, but at the time this parable was told Hades was an intermediate state where both the righteous and the wicked waited their final judgment and disposal.

The Book of Enoch describes Hades as consisting of four caves. Three were dark, gloomy, dry places where fire was continually burning. The other cave for the righteous was bright with growing flowers and there was a well or an everlasting spring there. This would account for Dives asking Lazarus to dip his finger in the spring and touch his tongue with the cool clear water. It was also true, according to rabbinical teachings, that the condemned and the saved could see each other in the afterlife as our story assumes.[5]

An interesting detail of the story is that Dives not only sees Lazarus at Abraham's side but he recognizes him. He even calls him by name. This would suggest that Dives was aware of Lazarus lying at his gate. He was not just a nameless beggar, but someone Dives had seen waiting at his gate for the scraps of food he could feed on.

Now even though the concept of Hades was that of an intermediate state that followed death but preceeded judgment, our parable assumes a finality about the state of Dives and Lazarus. However, closer reading of the story would suggest that the finality refers not to the status of Dives and Lazarus, but to the separation that divides them. "Besides all that, there is a deep pit lying between us, so that those who want to cross over from here to you cannot do so, nor can anyone cross over to us from where you are" (verse 26). Dives appeals to Abraham as the custodian of Hades to permit Lazarus to bridge this separation. He asks for very little — not a deluge, just a drop of water for his burning tongue. Abraham's answer is friendly but final. The bliss of Lazarus and the punishment of Dives is justified. As

154

they were separated in this life, so they are separated in the next. The conditions of life are reversed in the afterlife but the judgment is irrevocable and the separation is fixed and final. The rich experience poverty and pain. The poor experience blessings and comfort, and that is the way it is.

Many interpreters such as Julicher[6] and R. Bultmann[7] have understood the parable as offering a word of comfort to the poor. In their misery they could look to the future when they would get all the things they had been denied in this world. Now such a parable about the reversal of a rich and a poor man's destiny would have been certainly welcomed in first century Palestine. Josephus points out that just before the fall of Jerusalem there was civil rebellion of the lower classes in the city. The poor people revolted against the poverty thrust upon them by the rich and the ruling classes. Mobs rioted in the streets, plundered the houses of the rich and burned public buildings. Therefore, the first act of the parable would have been extremely popular among the masses as it spoke to a current social problem that needed attention.

Heaven and Hell

The parable of Dives and Lazarus has frequently been used as the basis for sermons about the rewards of heaven and the punishments of hell, the assumption being that knowledge of consequences will change people from their evil ways. Such preaching, however, is generally self-destructive. For if you succeed in convincing people of the desirability of heaven they will love God not for himself but for what they can get out of him. And at the same time preachers have made hell so horrible that they literally frighten hell right out of people. The view of hell becomes so distorted as to become unbelievable.

When you examine the plot of the story it fails to support such appeals and warnings. Dives wanted someone to return to his father's house and to his five brothers and warn them. In our words, preach a hell-fire and brimstone sermon to them. But Abraham's answer is that it wouldn't do any good. "If they will not listen to Moses and the prophets, they will not be convinced even if someone were to rise from death." The five brothers of Dives and Dives himself knew the consequences of their actions. They knew Moses represented the coded law and the certainty of justice with its rewards and penalties. And they knew that the prophets represented concern for a law above the law, justice, mercy and faith, which gave vitality to the dead letter of the law and activated the conscience. Nobody knew better than Dives that Moses and the prophets had long since been repudiated by his five brothers. Poteat, looking into the minds of Dives and his five brothers writes, "Had Moses and the prophets lived as they lived, they had laughingly said, they too would have been sensualists! It was the wilderness and the bitter land and hard living that gave the ancient moralists their notions about life. Their authority was as dead as their voices. Other times, other laws. And when Dives, fully aware of this, appealed to Abraham to perform a bizarre bit of magic to shock his brothers — a dead man to come back with a living message — it was Abraham this time who vetoed the suggestion. It was not a question of what voice would be authoritative; the simple fact was that no voice would be heard."

The parable teaches that knowledge of consequences will not really change people. You can in some cases change the way they live. They will make an effort to do certain things and avoid others to get to heaven and avoid hell, but they themselves will not be changed. They will be the same self-centered individuals as they were before. Only now they will adopt the attitude that it is to their advantage to be good in order to get to heaven in the end. Such goodness is distasteful to the Lord. It is the goodness of the mercenary. It is the goodness of the statistical saint who carefully counts his many blessings but at the same time keeps one eye on the good deeds he has done to make sure that the good works and blessings balance out.

The threat of hell and the reward of heaven never create the kind of Christian Christ desires. God is not a merchant selling passage into heaven, nor is he a judge rewarding the winner with a prize at the end of the race. Rather he is a father whose only desire is that his children love him freely and spontaneously without any thought of rewards or punishment.

Evils of Wealth

The "evils of wealth" has been a popular interpretation of this parable. The early church father Basil[8] said that the rich man was fried in the fire not because of his treatment of Lazarus but because of "his luxurious life." Some scholars note that the parable of Dives and Lazarus follows Luke's statement (verse 14) that, "The Pharisees heard all this (Jesus' statement concerning the making of friends by worldly wealth) and they made fun of Jesus because they loved money." In the light of this setting they view the parable as a lesson warning the Pharisees about the evils of wealth. Money, the parable teaches, both creates Lazaruses and ignores them.

However, the majority of interpreters maintain, it is not money in and of itself, or the possession of great wealth that is evil, but what wealth does to the person possessing it. Riches cause a person to become indifferent to human need. Money hardens the heart and blinds the eyes. It is like a mirror. A mirror is just a piece of clear glass that could be used as a window pane through which the whole world could be seen. But when a coat of silver is placed on that window glass, all that can be seen is the reflected image of yourself.

Insensitivity

Wallace sees the poor in need as the means by which we serve God.[9] Dives went to hell not because of his ill-treatment of the underprivileged at his gate, but because he did nothing to change their condition. Dives was not so much an evil man but an insensitive one. His was the sin of omission, not commission. He might have been a loving and considerate man to his family and friends, but he failed to love the unlovely. Dives did not possess the kind of love God has for the unlovely of this world that changes the conditions of the ones loved. Dives had with his wealth the power to alter the plight of the desperate victims of poverty, but he did nothing.

As pointed out above, there is no evidence that Dives was mean or cruel to Lazarus. He did not drive the beggars from his gate, which many men in his position had the reputation of doing. He showed charity to the needy but he made no effort to change their condition in life.

Voobus follows this same line of interpretation when he presents the point of the parable as being the fact that the only security, temporal and eternal, lies in togetherness.[10] Voobus adds the note that here Jesus is once more presenting his **new view of worship.** A right relationship among people is above all ceremonial worship. We now worship God as we serve those who are in need. The folly of Dives is precisely the fault of the goats on the left hand in the parable of the Sheep and the Goats. "I was hungry and you gave me no food." Dives made a goat out of himself by failing to be concerned for the beggars at his gate. And goats cannot pass through the gates of heaven.

This same social-service interpretation of the parable

greatly influenced the life of Albert Schweitzer. In fact, he identifies it as the decisive turning point of his life. While studying this parable he saw Lazarus as the needy continent of Africa lying at the gate of wealthy Europe. The rich nations passed by these underprivileged and poverty-stricken peoples as they amassed their vast colonial fortunes. As he continued to study the parable Schweitzer felt called to go forth into the dark continent to bring light and life to the needy Lazaruses of Africa.

"Remember My Son"

Poteat, in a very fresh approach to this social interpretation of the parable, zeroes in on the conversation between Dives and Abraham and particularly on the statement of Abraham, "Remember my son . . . " Dives is pictured in the parable as a sensualist. Now it is true that we are all sensualists. We could not live without our senses. "We are all endowed with normal appetites that must be satisfied." Undoubtedly Lazarus had the same sensuous desires as Dives. The difference was that with Lazarus they were frustrated, whereas with Dives they were satisfied.[11] If Lazarus could have changed places with Dives he would have jumped at the chance. He was not a religious ascetic voluntarily giving up the things of this world to purify his soul and earn a place in the bosom of Abraham. Given the opportunity Lazarus would have been delighted to strut down the streets of Jerusalem in the finest linen clothes money could buy. And if he had the cash he would have given banquets for his friends to rival any king's table. But he did not because he could not. Lazarus was poor not from choice but from circumstances. Many writers give the impression that there is a virtue in poverty and that Lazarus was a saint simply because he was poor. Nothing could be farther from the meaning of the story Jesus told.

The special tragedy of Dives is not that he was a sensualist; we all are, even the most righteous of us. Rather, according to Poteat, the tragedy of Dives is that his sensual pleasures caused him to **forget**.[12] Dives would have been an evil man even by his own standards if, seeing Lazarus at his gate he had driven him away, or even failed to do anything about his poverty. But this is precisely what he does not do. Rather, the sinful solution of Dives is to **not see him**, to not think about the poor at his gate but simply forget that they are there. The tragic truth is that no amount of deliberate blind forgetfulness can alter the situation at our gates.

One of the main lessons of this parable is that the time will come when we can no longer forget but will be forced to remember, but then it will be too late. According to Poteat, "The heaven of the sensualist, if he were to take time off from his sumptuous living to think about it, is the land where no evil thoughts molest, the land of glad forgetting."[13] This parable presents an opposite view of heaven and pictures it dramatically as a place of **remembering**. And the irony of the story is that the very person that he so easily forgot at his gate was his only hope of getting a drop of water to cool his tongue in the world to come.

The parable says to us that when sensual satisfaction of desires becomes an end in itself, it becomes a disease that blinds and deafens us. We live only for the pleasure of the moment and forget everything else. It is this forgetting that is deadly and betrays us in our death. But we need not wait for heaven to remember and to shake our eyes open; we can become awake here and now.

God calls us not to deny our senses but to use them. God calls us in this parable to be good sensualists. He calls us to use our senses not only to gratify our own pleasures but to make ourselves aware of the needs of others. There is nothing wrong with eyes that take pleasure in beautiful things such as purple garments and fine linen clothes, as long as we are not blinded to the fact that our brothers are forced to dress in rags. There is nothing wrong in enjoying a sumptuous meal as long as we do not forget that thousands suffer malnutrition and die of starvation. It is not our senses that destroy and condemn us but our memories. When we forget, we live with hell about us and think that it is heaven, but when we remember the needs of those about us, we take the first important step to improving situations — of transforming hells into heavens. For the very senses that blind and condemn us can also stir us to forceful actions of service and reform.

Review

These social-service interpretations of the parable have merit when considering only the first act or part of the parable. As we will point out later, Jesus adds to the parable of Dives and Lazarus a second act or story, and in the light of the rule of "end stress" the real lesson he intended for his listeners is to be found in this addition to the original parable.

Counterpoint

The interpretations that the parable is a social or moral teaching warning against the evils of wealth or indifference to human needs is a natural reaction because as listeners to the parable we tend to be influenced by the New Testament mind-set where love for the unlovely and service to the needy are dominant in the teaching. We easily read this love and service motif into the parable.

However, when the story is permitted to speak for itself, it does not say, as in the story of the Good Samaritan, that Dives passed by the poor man and ignored him. This is assumed, but this assumption is unwarranted in the light of the structure of the story. Important actions are seldom assumed in a story — they are stressed. The fact that Dives was indifferent and ignored Lazarus is never mentioned.

The story's main concern is the state or condition of the characters — a very rich man and a very poor man. What they did because of their economic status is not included in the story. The major contrast is who they are — not what they did. When Dives ends up in hell Abraham does not say, "You are here because you mistreated or even ignored the poor at your gate." Rather Abraham says, "Remember, my son, that in your lifetime you were given all the good things while Lazarus got all the bad things." The issue of the story is the contrast between the "haves" and the "have nots."

Even in the second act when Dives asked that his brethren be warned there is no indication of what they are to be warned of. If service to the needy and the poor had been the issue, it would seem that a good storyteller would have made clear and concise the nature of the warning. Since nothing is mentioned, the only thing they are guilty of is their great amount of riches.

The Second Act

The second act makes it quite evident that the parable is not primarily concerned with the reversal of fortunes after death, or indifference to the poor and needy, or the evils of wealth, or even the destiny of heaven and hell. If the story ended with the first act (verse 26) such conclusions might be valid, but it doesn't. Jesus goes on to present the second act of the parable and this is decisive for its meaning. Jeremias comments, "Since the first part is drawn from well-known folk-material, the emphasis lies in the new 'epilogue' which Jesus added to the first part."

Dives and Abraham

The main characters in the first act are Dives and Lazarus, but in the second act the main characters become Dives and Abraham. The whole drama now centers about a conversation. As Dives talks with Abraham we can see a plot parallelism. The parallel story is the Jewish race in conflict with its religious heritage. This is not to imply that allegorically Dives is the Jewish race and Abraham the religious heritage of the Jews. But as we hear the parable we can compare it to what was currently happening in the minds of the people as they struggled with the claims Jesus was making of his divine nature and status in relationship to the coming of the Kingdom of God.

In a series of requests Dives presents his grievances to father Abraham. The first request is minor, just a drop of water on his tongue to ease the pain. Likewise the Jews were always complaining from the time they fled from Egypt that they were the chosen people and still had to suffer in the wilderness, be tormented by their pagan neighbors, and finally had to live under the bondage of Roman rule. They were a people of much adversity and they needed at the very least a drop of mercy to ease their painful condition.

Then Dives politely asks that someone be sent to his father's house and warn his five brothers. This is a gentle way of pointing out that he had not been given fair treatment. If he had only received sufficient warning he would never have ended up in hell.

Many times Jesus had told stories about how the poor and the sinners would get into the Kingdom of God before the good Jews. Now he is telling a story that pictures the Jews ending up in hell while the poor and the sinners are in the bosom of Abraham. The Jews had heard Jesus but they had not believed him. The poor and the sinners welcomed what he had to say and gladly accepted it.

The excuse of Dives is that he had not been sufficiently warned. But the answer Abraham gives is that he had Moses and the prophets. This phrase "Moses and the prophets" means the rich religious heritage of the Jews. Abraham is saying that the heritage of the Jews is sufficient. Dives has no excuse nor do the Jews for failing to recognize Jesus as the Messiah.

Then Dives moves to the real issue of the parable, the key sentence that establishes the dramatic center of the plot. Dives says, "That is not enough!" Dives goes on to say, " . . . if someone were to rise from the dead." Scholars do not agree as to whether this is a reference to Jesus and his resurrection or not. Some even believe that it refers to Lazarus the brother of Mary and Martha whom Jesus raised from the dead. But this is not really important to the meaning of the parable. The essential issue is that Dives is asking for a special **sign** — an unusual event. He is asking for a sign that will be so obvious and apparent that no one would be able to avoid or deny it. By this request Dives is saying that his religious heritage — Moses and the prophets — is "not enough!"

Here we see in the story a plot parallelism with the continual struggle Jesus faced with the Jews who demanded of him a special sign. When Jesus presented his claim that he was sent from God and that he was bringing in the Kingdom of God, the Jews' response was always, "That is not enough! Show us a sign!"

At the beginning of his ministry Christ was tempted by the Devil to show forth special and dramatic signs of his Messiahship. His ministry ends with the mobs jeering him and crying out for special signs as he hangs on the cross. "If you are the son of God, come down from the cross." All his ministry between his baptism and his burial he was plagued by the Pharisees and the common man demanding, "That is not enough. Show us a sign!"

Jesus continued to refuse these demands for a special

sign, for he knew that God desired a faith relationship to exist between himself and his people. God does not want to force people to believe by glaring proof and spectacular acts, but by a word spoken in love. God spoke to his children through Moses and the prophets. He carefully prepared the way for the coming of the Messiah. But the Jews retort, "That is not enough! Give us a special sign!" They had turned the Law into a legal contract attempting to bind God to their good deeds. Now they were demanding of God a sign that would bind them to him. In the parable Jesus gives God's answer, "That is enough! Your religious heritage in Moses and the prophets is enough!" If the Jews — his people — cannot recognize the Messiah in the light of their rich religious heritage, then they will find themselves no longer blessed but their condition will be reversed and they will be condemned.

The meaning of this parable is simple and direct. God will give no special sign. The word of God in Christ and the heritage of Moses and the prophets is all they have and all they are going to get. That is enough!

Our Desire For Special Signs

Now what does this parable say to us? It says that we are not to demand or expect special signs from God. Rather we are to relate ourselves to God with trust and faith. We have been given his word — the Holy Scriptures — and his sacraments — baptism and communion — and they are sufficient. Nothing more will be given for nothing more is needed.

Some people will not believe for the word is not enough. They demand scientific proof and evidence of the incarnation, the virgin birth, the resurrection. They cannot accept events such as walking on the water, turning water into wine and raising of the dead. They will believe such events only when they can see them with their own eyes. Others want at least logical explanations that can be intellectually understood. They cry out in response to the efficacy of the word, "This is not enough." God presents his word and shares with us his sacraments and proclaims, "This **is** enough!"

Others say that the word and sacraments are not enough; we want an "inner feeling," a pentecostal experience where the Holy Spirit invades a person and he can really feel God's presence and be "born again." This parable says to such demands — "No! The word and the sacraments are sufficient! No such special signs will be given!"

Some people want a vision like a cross in the sky, a visiting angel or an audible voice undeniably calling them. Some just want special favors and then they will believe — restoration to health of a loved one, broken relationships restored, personal illness overcome, success in a venture, situations in life altered. To all such requests this parable says, "No! The word and the sacraments are all you need. No special signs will be given."

As Christ refused to give special signs to the Jews, so God refuses to give special signs to us today. We have the Word of God and the sacraments and together they are sufficient. We need nothing else. For faith is not a proved certainty beyond all shadow of doubt. Faith is believing what God says is true even when there is little evidence and no proof beyond the Word of God alone.

When Robinson Crusoe explored his lonely island there was no evidence of human life other than his own. Then he found one footprint in the sand. He recognized it was not his own and he had faith that there was someone else on the island. Despite all the evidence to the contrary that single footprint was enough for him to search until he found his friend Friday.

In the whole history of the world there is but one single footprint of God's presence in our world. A young

166

man, son of a carpenter, born in an obscure village, traveled only a few hundred miles, gathered about him a band of non-descript followers, taught simple stories about God's forgiveness and mercy, finally died on a criminal's cross and was buried in a borrowed tomb, his risen body viewed by a few nervous women and a few frightened men, yet that single footprint is enough! For millions of Christians that single nail-scarred footprint is sufficient for fantastic faith. For God speaks his word and says, "This is my son and your Savior," and that word is enough to change us and our world.

Notes

1. ArthurVoobus, **The Gospels in Study and Preaching**, (Philadelphia: Fortress Press, 1966), p. 33.
2. M. J. Ollivier, **The Parables of Our Lord**, (Richview Press Closkeagh: Browns and Nolan Limited, 1943), p. 198.
3. Voobus, op. cit., p. 36.
4. T.W. Manson, **The Sayings of Jesus**, (London: SCM Press, 1964), p. 296.
5. Voobus, op. cit., p. 37.
6. Adolf Julicher, **Die Gleichnisreden Jesu**, (Darmstadt: Wissenschaftliche Buchgesellschaft, 1963).
7 .R. Bultmann, **The History of the Synoptic Tradition**, ed. J. Marsh, (New York: Harper and Row, 1963). p. 196.
8. Basil, **Homiliae**, II MPG, 13, 213.
9. Ronald S. Wallace, **Many Things in Parables**, (New York: Harper and Brothers, 1955), p. 154.
10. Voobus, op. cit., pp. 46-47.
11. Edwin McNeill Poteat, **Parables of Crisis**, (New York: Harper and Brothers, 1950), p. 172.
12. Ibid., p. 173.
13. Ibid., p. 175.
14. Joachim Jeremias, **The Parables of Jesus**, (New York: Charles Scribner's Sons, 1955), p. 130.

*The
Divine
Human
Conductor*

8

THE PARABLE OF THE WIDOW AND THE JUDGE
Luke 18:1-8

The judge in this parable is called many things. Traditionally he is called the Unjust Judge. Filas[1] calls him "The Godless Judge." Hunter[2] refers to him as "The Callous Judge." Harvey[3] calls him "The Unrighteous Judge." C. W. F. Smith[4] calls him "The Unworthy Judge," and Eta Linnemann[5] refers to him as "The Unscrupulous Judge" and "The Impious Judge." The difficulty at arriving at an appropriate title for him is that according to the parable he was not really unjust and therefore the traditional title "The Unjust Judge" doesn't fit him. It is not accurate. In the story he does not pass down a bad decision. All the implications are that the widow's grievances were legitimate. The judge does not decide in favor of her adversary because he got a bigger bribe from him than he did from her. That would have been an injustice. No, when the judge finally acts in the story, he acts rightly and decides in her favor. The widow receives the justice she cries out for.

The point of the story is that the judge is reluctant to hear her case. He keeps putting her off. Therefore, the most descriptive title for the judge would be "The Unwilling Judge." However, even this title is not accurate, because the man really wasn't a judge as we think of a judge today. He was not the chief official of the court, sitting in black robes behind a bench of justice with a gavel of authority in his hand. He was a minor official in a local village. In a Jewish court at the time of Jesus, justice was not administered by one man but by a tribunal. The setting of our parable is much more informal and domestic than our common concept of a court of law. More than likely it took place in a small village where there was but one lawyer. According to Jewish law at the time when minor grievances of the law came up, any qualified lawyer could act as arbitrator between the two parties involved. Such service received no fee, but it was the responsibility of the lawyer to donate his services as a minor official of the court and settle the dispute. He judged the legality of the claims but he was not really a judge in our use of the word. Therefore, the best title we might give to this character in the story would be "The Unwilling Lawyer."

The title "widow" is also called into question. Some scholars such as Harvey point out that the term "widow" was a "byword for someone who was reduced to poverty through no fault of her own — had been the victim of some fraud or sharp practice."[6] So what we have is the story of an unwilling lawyer and a poor helpless client who has been the victim of fraud.

Two other matters need to be mentioned before we move into an interpretation of this parable. The first concerns the authenticity of the parable. Most scholars accept it as a parable Jesus told, but Eta Linnemann is certain we are not dealing with a parable of the historical Jesus. She says it is "a word of the ascended Lord, that is, a prophetic word that was spoken in the name and spirit of Jesus to the community of believers"[7] by some unknown narrator. In either case it is a word from God and we can take it seriously.

The second is the relationship of the introduction to the parable. The introduction states, "Then Jesus told them this parable to teach them that they should always pray and never become discouraged." Jeremias does not believe that this is "a correct indication of the aim of the parable."[8] This would mean that the parable is not necessarily about prayer. Rather, according to Jeremias, it is a vindication of the good news that God will eventually give judgment in favor of his elect which includes those who repent and turn to Christ.[9] The massive evidence of interpretations of this parable, however, indicates that most interpreters do focus in on prayer as the prime issue of the parable. Brunner, for example, includes it in his chapter entitled "Two Parables About Prayer."[10]

It would seem that there are three possibilities open to us. First we can follow the traditional interpretation of the parable and preach on the general **topic of prayer,** remembering that what is said here is not the total teaching of the New Testament concerning prayer, but only an important aspect of it. Secondly, we can approach the text as an **example story** — focus in on the actions of the widow and her persistence in prayer. Or thirdly, we can approach the story as a **contrast parable** and place our attention on the judge as an example of what God is not. This threefold scheme we shall observe in the discussion which follows.

The Great Two-Handed Engine
(A Parable About Prayer)

The first approach is to see the total text as a teaching concerning the general topic of prayer. John Milton has poetically described prayer as "the great two-handed engine." By this he means prayer is power. As Lord Tennyson said, "More things are wrought by prayer than this world dreams of." But it is a power not to get what we want, but to become the person God intends us to be.

The topic of prayer is too big to be dealt with in this discussion. However, a few suggestions might be helpful as a starter.

First, God may not always answer prayers but he always answers people. We may not always get what we want, but we always get what we need. God will not always eliminate disruptive disturbances and perplexing problems from our lives, but he will give us the power and the courage needed to endure them. God always listens to our prayers but his response may sometimes be "No!" As Eta Linnemann puts it, "God is not a slot-machine in which one only needs to insert the coin of persistent prayer to get what is wanted."[11]

Secondly, prayer is a relationship with God. It is a way of living before God. God governs our personal lives and the totality of existence according to his plan and will. Prayer is the means by which God includes us in the process of his plan.

Prayer is not so much getting what we want from God but relating ourselves to him. Prayer is not a means to an end; it is a means which is an end in itself. The content is not the important aspect of our prayers; rather, it is the act of praying that is important. Take a cross-word puzzle, for example. The easiest way to fill in the answers would be to wait until the next day's newspaper comes and see what the correct answers are. But this would destroy the whole fun of solving the puzzle. It is the process of working out the answers that gives meaning to the whole process of puzzle solving. So with prayer. The important thing is not what we ask or what we receive but it is the process of praying itself.

Or take a football game, for example. If the object is simply to get the ball over the goal line, then why not do it at night before the opposing team arrives? But that's not the point. It is the game, the activity, the involvement, the struggle, the tension that makes football what it is. So prayer is an activity, a struggle, by which God involves us in the game of faith relationships.

God knows what we want and need even before we ask. And he will give us what we need whether we ask or not. But he desires to include us in the process of his giving. On my way home from class one day I saw a student raking leaves in his back yard and then carrying them in huge bags to the front street. As the student came around the corner of the house, behind him came his three-year-old son. In his tiny fist he had a few little leaves. He was helping his father. True, his contribution amounted to nothing so far as the total job was concerned. The job could have been accomplished just as well without his help. But think what it meant to that little fellow to feel he was helping his dad and had a share in the job of cleaning up the yard. So with prayer. It lets us in on the process of God's giving to man. It does not decisively contribute to the process, for as stated above God will give whether we ask or not, if that giving is part of his plan. But prayer is the means by which God includes us in the process, and thereby we grow in our relationship to God.

Prayer is a kind of spiritual exercise that gives muscles to our faith. Like participation in sports you get the same amount of exercise when you win as when you lose the game. So prayer establishes and maintains a vital relationship with God when our prayers are answered and when they are not.

Therefore, prayer is not so much a means of getting what we want or need, but it is a process whereby God makes us into the types of persons God desires us to be.

The third suggestive idea about prayer in general is that it is not primarily a means by which we manipulate the will of God but discover it. So often our attitude in prayer is only the adequate expression of our own little wills, rather than a sincere desire to discover the will of God. Christ here is our example as he prayed in the Garden of Gethsemane. He did not struggle until perspiration dropped from his forehead like blood in a persistent effort to change the will of God for his life, but to discover what God's will **was** for his life. So prayer should be more like a question rather than a request. "Lord, what is thy will for my life?" And then wait patiently for his answer.

Prayer Is for the Stout-Hearted
(The Parable as Example Story)

Now let us look at the parable as an example story. Here we have a woman who is determined and persistent. She will not give up. She is stout-hearted, to say the least. She knows what she wants and she goes after it.

This persistence should not be interpreted as nagging God or making a nuisance of oneself with lengthy unending prayers until God is worn down to the point where he gives up, gives in, and gives the pray-er what he asks. Rather, what we see here is a courageous woman who is not afraid to stand up for her rights. She wants justice and she is obstinate about it.

So often we have an over-pious view of prayer. We are not actually honest in our prayers. We think certain things in our minds but we never open up and express them to God. We have doubts. We think that sometimes God is unfair and unjust. We disagree with what is happening and we feel God has a hand in it, but we are afraid to express these thoughts openly in our prayers. They are too unholy! Now this is foolish because God knows our thoughts whether we express them or not. But it is even more foolish because many times the only way we can come to know the faults and fallacies of our thoughts and wills is to openly and honestly share them with God. Ideas and thoughts are best dealt with in the open, be they good or bad thoughts.

God does not condemn honest conflict. As Jacob wrestled with the angel until he was blessed and as our Lord cried out from the cross, "Why hast thou forsaken me?", so God desires that we honestly express our thoughts, our doubts and disagreements with him. So many of us dress up our prayers as we dress up our children for Sunday School, all scrubbed and cleaned, polished and pressed. Our prayers sound nice. They are polite and holy but they are so often dishonest because they really don't express what we think or feel. If the woman in our parable can teach us anything at all, it is the true meaning of persistence in our prayer life. The secondary meaning of persistence is "continuing," but the primary meaning is "unyielding," "steadfast," "Single-mindedness." It is to be courageously insistent, actually demanding. Poteat finds the main lesson of this parable to be, "If you believe in the righteousness and justice of your cause, don't give up." When the prayer situation becomes tight with tension, we should not quit cold, but go on with an ardor that increases the longer one's ends are denied. Times were tough when Jesus told this parable. And he told it to those who had everything against them. They were to hold on, and fight until their unwearied quest was turned into victory.

Now this may sound strange when applied to prayer, but such insistence and steadfastness is what God desires if it is courageous and honest. For God cannot deal with our faults and fallacies until we declare them openly before him. God is not afraid of our doubts and demands. He is not shocked when we say to him, "God, I don't like what you are doing!" God welcomes such courageous honesty and he is well up to dealing with it. He will meet us blow-for-blow, and because he is God, he will win. But we will be the stronger in our faith for having lost this prayer-battle with our God.

How often in a good cowboy movie does the hero win over the town bully only after a rough-and-tumble, knock-down-drag-out fight. The bully learns to respect the hero by being defeated by him. So in our relationship with God, we learn to respect the righteousness of his will only when we challenge it and thereby discover in a most convincing way the weakness and the wrongness of our own wills.

This is the type of persistence that God wants in our prayer life — the persistence of this little widow who, knowing her cause was right, stood up courageously and fought until she was either defeated or satisfied. We may not always get what we want, but one thing is certain — God will get what he wants — people and not puppets.

How Much More
(A Parable of Contrast)

So far we have looked at the parable as a parable about prayer, and as an example story about being persistent in our praying. The approach that should be avoided when dealing with this passage is giving the implication to the listeners that the parable presents a sure-fire technique for successful praying. It is not a parable about how to win God and influence salvation. It is rather an invitation to pray honestly and courageously; it is the promise that God hears and answers prayers.

One way of avoiding the dangerous implication of techniques for praying is to view the parable as a *parable of contrast*. This interpretation places the focus of concern more on the judge than on the widow.

As we have pointed out above, the judge was not a judge in our common use of the word. He was a lawyer who acted as arbitrator in minor grievances that might arise in the village. The story presents him as a man "who neither feared God nor respected men." He creates the plot of the story by refusing to hear the pleas of a widow for justice. Now why he kept putting her off we can only speculate. Since he was not paid for settling minor legal suits, he may have ignored the widow because she was poor and he knew he could expect no "under-the-counter" gift of appreciation from her. It may be that he was bitter because he had to perform such legal services and this was his way of protesting what he thought was an injustice to himself. Or he might just have been lazy. But no matter what reason he might have had, the story makes it quite clear that the lawyer kept putting the widow off and refused to hear her case.

Everything was against the widow. Her adversary was ruthless, her friends were not there to help, and she could not appeal to the religious, humane or moral sensibilities of the lawyer. In the process of the parable, the lawyer-judge is not converted nor does he change. He is the same indifferent character at the end of the story as at the beginning. Now the widow knew that he cared not for God or man but she was smart enough to know that he cared for himself. So she went back to him again and again and finally for his own peace of mind he granted her request, as we might give a quarter to a bum, not to help him, but to get rid of him.

The lawyer-judge is pictured as a man who cares nothing whatsoever for the woman and her problems. He serves her, but he has no compassion for her as a person nor any sympathy for her cause.

Jesus then draws the contrast. God is not like this indifferent, unwilling lawyer-judge. God hears his people and judges in their favor. And, Jesus adds, God is not like **this** judge because he is not "slow to help them, I tell you he will judge in their favor, and do it quickly."

This would seem to preclude the necessity of persistence in our prayer life as the point of the parable. We may need persistence when dealing with an indifferent and unwilling earthly judge, but not when we deal with God, for he judges in our favor — **quickly!**

Justice

When this parable is held up to the total teachings of the New Testament, we also see that it has something to say to us concerning justice. Whereas the lawyer-judge in the parable is unwilling to help, God is concerned and eager to come to our aid. Whereas the lawyer-judge is interested in bribes, God is concerned that we bring nothing to him but our problems.

The picture the New Testament gives concerning justice is not a client in search of a lawyer to defend him as in the parable, but a defense attorney in search of clients who are in need. The parable ends up not on the note of man's persistence, but on the **promise** of God's determination to help us, to judge in our favor and to do it quickly.

Will He Find Faith?

One more point needs to be considered before we leave this text, and that is the statement that Christ makes at the conclusion of the parable, "But will the Son of Man find faith on earth when he comes?"

The question this raises is how does Jesus get the concept of faith out of this parable? To answer this, we need to take the idea of faith back to the story of the parable and when this is done an interesting insight emerges. The widow in the story has a tremendous need and she has no one to help her. She lives in a small village in which there is only one lawyer. He alone can help her, but he is unwilling. There is nowhere she can turn for help. There is no one to whom she can plead her case. She is helpless so she must somehow work out her own salvation. So she sets out and by her own persistence wins.

When we place this over against the situation at the time of Jesus, we see a plot parallelism in the Jews who found themselves in a similar situation. They viewed God as an indifferent and sometimes unwilling judge before whom they had to work out their own salvation by their persistence in prayer and many good works.

Christ comes bringing a new view of God and justice. God is not indifferent and unwilling; he is rather an aggressive giver of grace and justice. Therefore, man is no longer helpless; he has a helper. And we need no longer, like the widow, work out our own salvation. We not only have a good judge but a devoted and dedicated defense attorney come from God. We have only to surrender to him in faith and our needs will be met and we will be saved.

This, then, is the stinging issue presented by the parable — will we, like the helpless widow, before an unwilling judge trust in our own good works and persistently attempt to work out our own salvation, or shall we take a stand of faith knowing that we have help in an advocate, a vindicator, a savior? Will we trust in God and God alone knowing that he is a loving and concerned father who stands ready to grant us all we need even before we ask?

Jesus therefore asks, "Will the Son of Man find **faith** on earth when he comes?" Will he find men like the helpless widow still striving to work out their own salvation, or will he find men standing steadfast in the faith that their salvation is in Christ, and Christ alone? Once more we see the triumph of grace over good works.

During World War I a young communications officer was sent out onto the battlefield to repair a broken telegraph line. When he arrived at the point of the break in the line, he saw the two wires dangling in a tree. When he had climbed the tree and was ready to make the repair, a shell exploded nearby, riddling his body with schrapnel. He was dying and knew that he didn't have enough time or strength left to repair the line. So in those last few moments of his life, he made a desision and with one hand he grabbed hold of one end of the line, and with the other hand he grabbed hold of the other end of the line — and the current **flowed**. His body had become a human conductor and the current flowed.

So Christ, facing our helpless condition as lost and separated from our God, went to a cross. And there, with arms outstretched, he grabbed hold of God with one hand, embraced us with the other, and the current flowed.

The parable of the widow, alone and helpless before the unwilling judge, stands in direct and glaring contrast to our position in faith. For we stand not before an unwilling God, but a God of grace and goodness. And we stand not helpless and alone, but are embraced by an heroic advocate who will plead our case and win for us salvation.

Notes

1. Francis L. Filas, **The Parables of Jesus,** (New York: Macmillan, 1959), p. 82.
2. Archibald M. Hunter, **The Parables Then and Now,** (Philadelphia: Westminster Press, 1971), p. 81.
3. A. E. Harvey, **Companion to the New Testament,** (Oxford: Oxford University Press, 1971), p. 274.
4. Charles W. F. Smith, **The Jesus of the Parables,** (Philadelphia: United Church Press, 1975), p. 183.
5. Eta Linnemann, **Jesus of the Parables,** (New York: Harper and Row, 1964), p. 120.
6. Harvey, op. cit., p. 274.
7. Eta Linnemann, op. cit., p. 121.
8. Joachim Jeremias, **Rediscovering the Parables,** (New York: Charles Scribner's Sons, 1966), p. 77.
9. Ibid., p. 116.
10. Emile Brunner, **Sowing and Reaping,** (Richmond, Va.: John Knox Press, 1946), p. 84.
11. Eta Linnemann, op. cit., p. 123.

Justification
By
Faith
Jesus-Style

9

THE PARABLE OF THE PHARISEE AND THE PUBLICAN
Luke 18:9-14

This is the story of two men who did the right thing at the right time in the right place, but one of them did it in the wrong way. A Pharisee and a publican went to the temple at the appointed hour and prayed. And the surprise is that the Pharisee who was trained and experienced in the art of praying was the one who did it the wrong way. But then this is not so surprising when we realize this is not a human evaluation of prayer we are dealing with, but God's. He looks at the heart. Before God there is neither Pharisee nor publican, neither good nor bad people, there is only honesty and hypocrisy. All men are sinners, the only difference is some admit it and others do not. And that is what this parable is all about. The Pharisee was so proud of his goodness and righteousness that he was blind to the fact that he was still a sinner. The publican on the other hand was so disgusted with his life, and the way he lived it that the only recommendation concerning himself he could bring to God was the fact that he was a sinner. Yet Jesus says that the Pharisee was wrong; the publican alone went home right with God. Eta Linnemann warns us that the interpretation we give this parable is determined in advance because of the effect this story has had in Christian tradition. The Pharisee is the symbol for hypocrisy, pride and pompous piety. The publican wears the halo of the ideal type of humble sinner. Linnemann then points out that, "If we want to understand the story aright, we must abandon this prejudgment and try to listen to the story as Jesus' listeners must have understood it."[1] Therefore, let's begin by looking at these two men and where they came from in more detail.

The Pharisee

First, the Pharisee. We know that he was a pious man in his daily living. He knew the Law and lived it. He was a hardworking churchman. If anything was to be accomplished in the church, the cooperation of the Pharisee was indispensable. He was a Biblical fundamentalist. He read and studied the scriptures and believed every word of them. But even more important, he was not ashamed of the scriptures; he talked about them constantly. He was a missionary. The Jewish communities scattered around the Mediterranean world were the results of the efforts of the Pharisees.

What is often overlooked concerning the Pharisees is the great religious heritage in which they stood. Religion before the giving of the Mosaic Law was purely ritualistic. It consisted primarily of the rite of the cult, sacrifice and worship, and had little to do with the everyday lives of the people. With the coming of the Law, religion became socialized and more humanized. The Ten Commandments dealt with the interpersonal relationships not only between God and the people, but also between the people with one another. Of all the groups or divisions within Judaism, the Pharisees understood this new element that had entered the development of religious thought. They applied religion to the everyday life of the people. True, they multiplied and applied the Law to a ridiculous extreme. They ended up overdoing a good thing and made a profession and a public performance out of personal piety, but nevertheless more than anyone else — including the prophets — the Pharisees were responsible for the personal and social aspects of Jewish faith.

Second, it was the Pharisees who developed the

rabbinical system in Judaism. The first teachers and the first efforts at pastoral ministry were begun by the Pharisees. The priests served in the temple, but the Pharisaic rabbis served the people in their daily needs.

Third, it was the Pharisees who established and maintained the synagogue with its emphasis on knowledge of the scriptures. The institution of the synagogue enabled the Jewish people to survive the persecution and the captivity of dispersion. They, more than any other group, were responsible for maintaining intact the Holy Scriptures down through the troubled times of Jewish history.

There is little doubt that the Pharisees were true religious heroes of the faith and stood in an honored tradition. So often we hear about the prophets, but without the Pharisees we would have no social concept of the ministry, no pastors, no Sunday School and no Bible. They were truly heroes of the faith, but they were heroes with clay feet. For by the time of Christ they had managed to corrupt the great contributions of their heritage. They were misusing their knowledge of scriptures to establish their own authority and religious superiority. They who had once brought religion to the people were now by their excessive interpretations taking religion from the people.

Perhaps this is why Jesus singled out the Pharisees and was so energetic in his criticism of them. They had so much that they could have offered to the people, but they were so blatantly betraying their great religious heritage and tradition.

At the time of Christ the Pharisees were a very popular and powerful party within society. Many of them were uneducated common people, but their leaders, known as scribes, were some of the most educated men of the Jewish community. In the realm of religious matters, the Pharisaic Party was supreme. The liturgy used by the priests was ordered and governed by Pharisaic law.

The Sadducees who believed in the Torah, or the written law only, were completely powerless before the Pharisees. The Pharisees represented the great middle class people and were commonly referred to as the "People's Party." The Pharisees fought on two fronts. They opposed the Sadducees and the aristocrats on the one hand and the publicans and the sinners on the other. The ordinary Jew looked to the Pharisee as the model of Jewish tradition, personal piety and educated wisdom. The Pharisees represented the embodiment of the ideal life.

Little Jack Horner

The Pharisee in the parable Jesus told is hardly recognizable as being a member of the glorious tradition of the Pharisaic movement we have just considered. He is an over-drawn caricature of a self-righteous man. His personality is so exaggerated that he reminds one of Little Jack Horner who sat in the corner saying, "What a good boy am I." In just two sentences he mentions himself six times. "I thank you, God, that I am not greedy, dishonest or immoral like everybody else. I thank you that I am not like that tax-collector. I fast two days every week, and I give you one-tenth of all my income." Chapel says, "He had a good eye on himself, a bad eye on his neighbor, and no eye on God."

Barclay is impressed by the fact that the Pharisee is a man of negative goodness.[2] He does not stress what he has done but what he has **not** done. Even his fasting and his tithes are viewed not as positive offerings to God but as negative restraints. He was a good man but he was good for nothing.

He is also presented as a satisfied man. Clarence Jordan says that he asked nothing from God and he got nothing. He was a good man and he knew it. So he really didn't need God at all. But one of the most notorious traits, according to most interpreters, is that he elevated himself by downgrading his fellowmen. He promoted his virtues by pointing out the vices of others.

So the character of the Pharisee is presented as a self-centered man, satisfied with himself, negatively stressing his good points, and promoting himself at the expense of others. He should not be seen as the typical Pharisee but as a caricature carefully drawn by a masterful storyteller.

The Publican

In direct contrast to the Pharisee we have the publican. He, too, stands in a tradition, but it is not a noble one; it is a notorious one. He was a tax collector and in the days of Jesus they were no more popular than they are today. In fact, they were much less popular; they were hated and despised. Barclay refers to him as "the most hated man in town."

Roman taxes were of two types — direct (Property, poll, and income) and indirect (fees on sales and purchases, export and import customs). Instead of collecting indirect taxes through government officials, Rome auctioned the job out to rich contractors. These men were called "tax farmers." They divided their farm or territory into districts and employed local agents to do the actual work of collecting the taxes. These subagents were customs house officers who examined merchandise, assessed its value and exacted the taxes. The tax farmers were, in the strict sense, the publicans, for the Greek word used in the New Testament means literally to "farm taxes." But the word came to be loosely used for the subordinates and these are the "publicans" so frequently mentioned in the New Testament.[3]

The fact that the publican could arbitrarily set the tax led to flagrant injustices; therefore, the publicans were universally hated throughout the empire. The Jews had additional reasons for despising the publicans. They looked on taxes not as a necessary evil to preserve and maintain social order, but as tribute paid to a hated conqueror. And when a Jew accepted the job of publican he and his family were immediately despised by the whole community and excommunicated. He was no longer allowed in the temple or the synagogue, and his testimony was not acceptable in a court of justice. So far as the Jews were concerned the publican was not only a sinner but a heathen as well.

The Pharisee in our parable may not have adequately represented his noble tradition, but the publican certainly did represent his. The parable says, "Two men went up to the temple to pray." It does not say that both entered the temple. Undoubtedly the publican was aware that his profession prohibited him from entering the sacred precincts. The parable carefully makes this clear by saying, "But the tax collector stood at a distance." J. Stanley Glen plays on this fact of the distance between the Pharisee and the publican and entitles his chapter on this parable "The Insider and the Outsider."[4] Glen sees the Pharisees in the church today. They are the ones who feel they have a monopoly on the presence and favor of God, but who actually are separated from God because of their egotism and self-righteousness. There are also publicans within the church. They are the ones who are inside the church physically but really "outsiders" so far as a fellowship of kindred spirits is concerned. They know the subtle, silent treatment that speaks more loudly than words that they are not really active members of the church. They are never asked to do anything in the church, serve on committees or take responsibilities. This leadership of the church is in the hands of a few pharisaic "pillars" who run the whole show. Glen concludes, "The gulf which separates the ancient Pharisee and the tax collector in the house of God will separate this 'outsider' from the 'insider' in the same place and manner."[5]

Eta Linnemann also sees within the parable a word to the interpersonal relationships within religion. The parable challenges the Jews to re-evaluate their standard concerning righteousness. If the standard is the Law as the measure of self-righteousness, then he who fulfills the Law can arrive at a good verdict concerning himself, but he excludes his neighbor who fails to fulfill the Law. On the other hand, if the grace of God is the standard, then he not only arrives at a good verdict concerning himself, but he includes his sinful neighbor as well.[6] Jesus tells this parable to the Jews that they might give up their exclusive dependence on righteousness by the Law, and become their brother's keeper. Jesus was appealing to the Jews to accept the responsibility for the sinners in their midst, and count on God's grace to save them all.

The parable according to Luke is directed to, "Those who trusted in themselves that they were righteous." Jesus by this parable says, "What about others? Are you not concerned for their salvation?" Here we see the new orientation toward salvation which Jesus brings. Up to this time the basic religious question was, "What must I do to be saved?" Jesus changes that question to, "What must I do, that others might be saved?" This is the decisive difference that the Gospel makes.

For example, if I truly believe that Christ has done everything for my salvation and there is nothing left for me to do, then when I get up in the morning I do not say to myself, "O.K. I have twelve hours today in which to serve and please God in order that he will judge me worthy of salvation." No, rather, free in the Gospel, I arise in the morning saying, "I am saved. I am certain of this because of Christ. Therefore I have twelve hours today to help others come to know and believe in Christ." The Gospel frees us **from** concern for ourselves, so we can be completely and totally free **to be** concerned for and to serve others. This is the radically new orientation Christ brings to religious faith — freedom **from** self **for** others.

So the publican stands before God crying out for mercy, but at the same time he stands before us. He needs our help and concern as well as God's. He needs to know that he is justified by God and it is our responsibility to witness to him, to go to him with the Gospel of Christ and assure him of his justification before God. Of this we will have more to say later.

The publican stood apart and beat on his breast — or to be more exact on his heart which, according to the New Testament is the seat of sin. This man is desperate. He does not lift up his hands in the usual gesture of prayer. In fact, his words are not really a prayer in the ordinary sense of the word. Rather they are a cry of despair. And Jesus adds that it is a cry to us as well as to God.

Many Interpretations

Many scholars begin their discussion of the parable of the Pharisee and the Publican with the statement that the meaning of this parable is so obvious and self-evident that they hesitate to waste another word upon it. However, this does not stop them and they proceed to discover within the story fresh and different insights that are stimulating and suggestive. Let us look at a few of the various treatments scholars have given to this parable which have not been included in our discussion above.

The Pride of a Pompous Pietist

Hunter believes the meaning of the story is simple. The trouble with the Pharisee is that he is good and knows it. "For when a man knows that he is righteous the odds are he is not."[7] Spurgeon once said that he thought a certain man in his congregation the holiest man he had ever known — till the man told him so himself!

Plumer agrees and adds that the phrase "stood apart by himself" really means "chose a conspicuous place" — a place where he was sure to be seen by other men. For he had not come to pray or give thanks to God but to congratulate himself personally.[8] "He glances at God but contemplates himself. Indeed he almost pities God who but for himself would be destitute of faithful servants." In the delightful children's poem on this parable Joann Scheck puts it this way:

Again that night the Pharisee
ate only water and some bread.
"How very happy God must be
to have a friend as good as me,"
he thought as he climbed into bed.[9]

The Snob Who Holds Others In Contempt

Granskou believes that the parable is directed against "the exclusive attitude" of religious insiders. The fault of the Pharisee was not his pride, but that his pride led him to looking down on and despising others.[10]

Poteat, following this same line, comments that both men went to the temple with conviction. One was convinced of his righteousness and the other of his sin.[11] Both men told the truth about themselves. According to Poteat this is the story of a righteous man that had become self-righteous: "The sure man has become the cocksure man; the self-reliant has become the snob."[12] Now snobbishness is tragic for it makes of a person a fraud. The person actually loses his self-reliance and must now rest his sense of worth on putting other people down. The greater his scorn of others the more secure he feels. He downgrades others in order to elevate himself. The greater the snob the more he must put up a false front. He must brag about his accomplishments not just to impress others, but to convince himself. This is brought out according to Poteat when Jesus says, "The Pharisee stood and prayed **with himself**." The problem of the Pharisee was not just his relationship to God but his relationship to himself. The publican left the temple with his problem on the way to being settled, but the Pharisee left the temple as he had entered it — insecure, uncertain, unconvinced that he was really good. He still had to prove to himself his own righteousness, so he continued playing the role of a pious man and saying to himself over and over again, "At least I am thankful I am not as bad as other men." His pride was his fraud and his protection from facing the fact of his own lack of righteousness. He was a victim of himself. Poteat sees this man as committing the unpardonable sin, "unpardonable, not because of the lack of God's effective grace, but because of its imperviousness to the moral insight that alone leads one to seek his grace and redemption."[13]

Cadoux comes to much the same conclusion concerning the Pharisee when he says, "The Pharisee's contempt for his fellowman makes his own soul impervious to God."[14] Cadoux sees this parable to be an illustration of the truth that there is nothing without a man, that entering him can defile him; but the things that come out of him, those are what defile a man.

The Pharisee came to the temple with a closed mind, not asking or seeking but telling God what a good man he was. The whole picture of his personality is **rigidity**. His life is closed tight.

This says something to those who wonder if going to church makes any difference. The answer is within ourselves. If we come to worship closed tight with pride and self-confidence like the Pharisee, then nothing will happen, because nothing can happen. God cannot fill hearts and hands that are tightly gripped closed. It is only when we open our hearts and hands, tear open our lives like the tax collector that God can enter in and fill us, change us, and work his miracle of growth within us. How we leave the church and its worship depends to a great extent on how we enter it. No man leaves the church and goes down to his house a new and better person unless he enters the church wanting and willing to be changed.

Bruce goes one step beyond the idea of contempt for fellowmen and sees Luke's universalist hand heavily at work within the parable. Because the Jews regarded the publicans as heathen the parable is directed to the universal application of the gospel. It is a parable of hope for Gentiles, that if they are penitent the Kingdom of God is for them as well as for the Jews.[15]

Faith With Dirty Hands

Wallace points out the radical new teaching which this parable presents. The Psalmist had asked the question, "Who shall ascend into the hill of the Lord? or who shall stand in his holy place?" And the answer he gave, every good Jew understood and accepted, "He that hath clean hands and a pure heart." Jesus defied this accepted teaching with his story about "a man with impure hands and an unclean heart, standing in the holy place before God, and accepted by God because of his faith."[16] Faith is the key word here. For faith is an approach to religion that looks away from the condition of man's hands to the condition of God's heart which is open to all those who call upon him for help. "Faith is the acknowledgement in the presence of the merciful God that everything outside of this mercy is a false and worthless foundation to build upon, and that this mercy alone can be the starting point of the entirely new life that is required if a man is to be saved."[17] This concept of faith as ceasing to trust in ourselves and throwing ourselves totally on the mercy of God was a strange

194

teaching to the Jews. The portrait of the Pharisee who lacked faith because he did not trust in the mercy of God alone, they could not understand. The Jews were hearing for the first time the gospel that men are justified by faith alone and they were rejecting it. So today many still find it impossible to give up confidence in their own selves and therefore it is impossible for them to have faith in God alone. Like the Jews they cannot accept a faith that welcomes people with dirty hands. And this can only mean that in the end they will reject a God who insists on washing men's dirty feet.

Strange New Standards

Thielicke finds in this parable the contrast of standards by which people judge themselves. "The Pharisee measures himself by looking downward."[18] He chooses the bad publican as a standard. This always produces pride. The publican measures himself "upward." "God Himself is his standard."[19] This always produces a sense of one's sinfulness. Here, according to Thielicke, we catch the very fine difference that distinguishes the way the Pharisee and the publican prayed. Then Thielicke adds the warning, "A false proud look at our neighbor can spoil everything for us and turn the grace of God into putrefaction."[20]

Degrees of Holiness

Filas takes the position that this is not a story about one man being justified before God and the other man not. Rather, it is a matter of degree. The Pharisee thought that his righteousness was better and superior to the publican and discovered that it was not. Filas suggests that, according to Aramaic, what Jesus said was, "This man (the publican) went back to his house justified **more than** the other."[21] Jesus is not disputing the fact that the Pharisee is holy, but he is pointing out that the publican, because of his acknowledged sinfulness, was more holy than the Pharisee. The lesson Jesus teaches here is that following the Law can produce holiness, but the flinging of oneself totally and completely upon the mercy of God is what truly makes one holy. For this holiness is not an accomplishment of a person, but a gift from God. This is a very fresh and stimulating interpretation and deserves more consideration of its preaching possibilities.

The Goodness of God

Jeremias sees this parable as one of many that presents the goodness of God. He points out that the prayer of the Pharisee is legitimate. For whereas the Law prescribes only one annual fast, he fasts voluntarily twice a week. And he gives tithes of everything he buys to make sure of using nothing that has not been tithed. "He offers God not only his person, but also his purse." The Pharisee makes no requests to God; he only offers thanks. Then Jeremias asks, "What fault can be found with his prayer?"[22]

Ollivier answers this question by stating his opinion that the Pharisee had not really done anything to brag about. The Pharisee fasts twice a week but he does this with ostentation which destroys its validity. He gives tithes not of what he possesses but of what he gains — his income. And Ollivier adds, these gains come "at the expense of the widows, whose artless piety he makes use of for his own advantage."[23] Ollivier bases this on Mark 12:40 where it is said of the teachers of the Law, "They take advantage of widows and rob them of their homes, then they make a show of saying long prayers."

The point would seem to be that whether one accepts the content of the Pharisee's prayer as valid or not, the motivation behind it is wrong, because he himself is

196

wrong. This is compounded by the fact that he fails to put his trust in God's goodness. The publican, on the other hand, is wrong but he throws himself on the goodness of God and wins the day.

Humility

In this brief survey of interpretations, it is interesting and perhaps surprising that none of them finds the parable to be a neat little moral lesson presenting the virtue of humility. This is particularly unusual if you read or listen to many sermons on this text, for in most cases humility has been the popular preacher's approach to this parable.

Now few would disagree that humility is a desirable virtue. And that it is certainly suggested within the structure of this story.

A young seminarian returned to his home congregation to preach the Sunday sermon. He was excited with the new insights he had learned the past year. He was full of higher and lower criticism of the scriptures and he looked forward to returning to his home pulpit and setting the record straight on a few decisive issues in the Bible. He wrote a sermon that he was certain was superior to anything his home congregation had ever heard. He walked into the pulpit with his dazzling new white alba. When the sermon hymn had finished, he opened his mouth but nothing came out, his mind went blank and his voice left him. He struggled for a few moments that seemed like hours and then in tears rushed from the pulpit. In the sacristy afterwards he pathetically asked his home pastor what had happened. The old pastor hesitated for a second and then he said, "Son, if you had entered the pulpit in the same spirit you left it, you would have preached a great sermon."

Now it is true that humility is an essential

characteristic of the Christian personality, particularly as we stand before God and serve his will. But humility is not something that can be preached to others as a duty or a requirement. For the moment we attempt to consciously accomplish humility we defeat our own efforts.

Like the old monk speaking about the virtues and the accomplishments of his order said, "Well, we are not an order of outstanding scholars, or skilled craftsmen, or great artists, but one thing you can say about our order, we **are** humble!"

If we use this parable to preach to our people that they should be humble like the publican and then God will bless them, then the same thing might happen to them that happened to the publican in a humorous sequel to the parable.

It seems that the publican heard Jesus tell the story of the Pharisee and the publican. He said to himself, "That's me he's talking about! What do you know? I'm famous! I'm the example of how all men should approach God and pray to him." So the next day the publican went to the temple. He looked around to see if anyone there recognized him. He beat on his breast and cried out, "Lord have mercy on me!" Then out of the corner of his eye he saw the Pharisee going through his daily prayers. And to himself the publican thought, "That pompous pious old fool, I'm glad I'm not like him!"

So preaching that exhorts people to be humble and presents it as a virtue to be sought after can only be self-defeating. Humility from the heart operates like good digestion in the stomach - when it is thought about the least! Humility is something that cannot be commanded. It cannot be sought after or striven for. Humility is something that happens when we stand in the presence of God and honestly see ourselves in the light of his holy righteousness. Humility is not a positive possession of the personality, but it is the emptiness one feels as we stand before perfection. When we totally forget ourselves

being captivated by the holiness of God, then and only
then are we truly humble. And like the publican there is
only one thing that we can say, "Lord have mercy upon
me."

To Be Justified Is Not Enough

One of the most stimulating and suggestive
interpretations of this parable comes from Bruce, who
begins by pointing out that the publican's account of
himself is correct. He is a sinner. The parable does not say
that he is a just man and the Pharisee is an unjust man;
rather it says "the publican is nearer the approval of God
than the other who approves himself."[24] The parable
must be seen in the Pauline understanding of
justification. Man is justified not because of his
character, the fact that he is good or bad, moral or
immoral, but man is justified by the relationship he has
with God. The publican stands in need of God and
therefore he is right with God. The publican left the
temple just as much a sinner, morally speaking, as when
he entered it. But he left a justified sinner. That is, he
left the temple as a sinner standing in a right
relationship with God. There is no indication in the story
that the publican left the temple feeling in his heart that
he had been forgiven. And the Pharisee more than likely
left the temple still pleased with himself. He had no idea
that he had failed to be justified and the publican had
succeeded. Justification as well as salvation is not
dependent on changing moods or how we "feel" inwardly.
It is God's judgment on us, **not** how we feel about
ourselves.

Wallace stresses this same thing when he warns his
listeners against placing too much stress on religious
feelings. The publican left the temple with no sweet
feelings of inward peace. But his heart lied to him and
his feelings deceived him. God had forgiven him but he

did not know it. "He stood justified before God yet he felt he was condemned."[25] We should therefore find assurance nowhere else except in "the thought of God's goodness and mercy, and no matter what we feel within ourselves, never take our eyes off Him who has been lifted up to draw us ever to Himself."[26]

Bruce points out that all we have in this parable is that it pleases God when we confess our sins and such confession places us in a right relationship to God. But we do not have here a complete statement concerning justification.[27] As said before, the publican went to his house justified in God's sight but not necessarily in his own. He had not "found peace," nor did he have any sense of "being born again," as these current phrases are used. The point is that the publican still needed to hear the word that he was saved. There is within the parable no word of absolution, no declaration of grace that the publican might hear, know and believe that he had been justified before God. He still needs a witness — one who will come to him and proclaim the truth of what has happened to him.

To us who stand on this side of the cross, the parable reminds us that we, too, have been declared righteous and justified by God. We, too, stand in a right relationship with God. Not, however, because of our humility or our desperate cry for mercy, but because of the humiliation of our Savior and his cry from the cross on our behalf. But like the publican in our story, we too need to hear, know and believe that we now stand justified in the sight of God. This is why the gospel is proclaimed to us and why we have a responsibility to proclaim it to others.

Several years ago a popular novel told the story of a girl who felt a responsibility to care for her family after her mother died. One day she fell in love with a young sea captain who asked her to run away with him and be married on board his ship. At first she could not answer him. She had to think it over. But she told him that if her answer was yes she would let him know before his ship sailed in the morning. That afternoon she decided and sat down and wrote a note confessing her love and her willingness to go with him anywhere in the world. As her brother was leaving the house she gave him the note to deliver to the captain. She went upstairs and packed her belongings. The next morning she waited. The morning passed and still she waited. Frantically she ran up the stairs and looked from the upper window, only to see her lover's ship sailing out of the harbor. For the years that passed she lived a bitter, lonely, disappointed life. Then several years later she was gathering up some old clothes for a church rummage sale and she found the coat her brother wore on that fateful day, and there in the pocket of his coat was her note of love still undelivered.

Our world is filled with bitter, lonely, disappointed people for whom life has little or no meaning, for they have never received the note of God's love and forgiveness. Like the neglectful brother, we carry this note around with us undelivered. It is not enough that God justifies the ungodly and that people are saved by faith — they must hear this good news. And we who have heard it have a responsibility to share it with others.

Our justification before God is not based on the fact that two men went to the temple and by their actions taught us how to approach God and pray. Rather our justification is based on the fact that one man went to a cross. There he did not so much teach us something by this act; rather, he **did** something for us. He did what no man can do for himself. By his precious blood and body he placed us clean and renewed into the presence of God our Father and we were pronounced — justified!

Notes

1. Eta Linnemann, **Jesus of the Parables**, (New York: Harper and Row,

1964), p. 58.
2. William Barclay, **The Gospel of Luke**, (Philadelphia: Westminster Press, 1956), p. 232.
3. **New Catholic Encyclopedia**, Vol. XI, (New York: McGraw-Hill, 1967), p. 1012.
4. J. Stanley Glen, **The Parables of Conflict in Luke**, (Philadelphia: Westminster Press, 1962), pp. 54-63.
5. Ibid., p. 63.
6. Linnemann, op. cit., p. 63.
7. Archibald M. Hunter, **The Parables Then and Now**, (Philadelphia: Westminster Press, 1971), p. 64.
8. Alfred Plumer, **The Gospel According to Luke**, International Critical Commentary XXVII, Ed. by C. A. Brigg, (New York: Scribner's and Sons, 1906), p. 417.
9. Joann Scheck, **The Two Men in the Temple**, Arch Books, (St. Louis: Concordia, 1968).
10. David M. Granskou, **Preaching on the Parables**, (Philadelphia: Fortress Press, 1972), pp. 105-106.
11. Edwin McNeill Poteat, **Parables of Crisis**, (New York: Harper and Brothers, 1950), p. 206.
12. Ibid., p. 209.
13. Ibid., p. 212.
14. A. T. Cadoux, **The Parables of Jesus**, (New York: Macmillan, 1931), p. 216.
15. A. B. Bruce, **The Parabolic Teachings of Christ**, (New York: George H. Doran, 1886), p. 313.
16. Ronald S. Wallace, **Many Things in Parables**, (New York: Harper and Brothers, 1955), p. 102.
17. Ibid., p. 101.
18. Helmut Thielicke, **The Waiting Father**, (New York: Harper and Brothers, 1959), p. 131.
19. Ibid., p. 134.
20. Ibid., p. 136.
21. Francis L. Filas, **The Parables of Jesus**, (New York: Macmillan, 1959), p. 86.
22. Joachim Jeremias, **Rediscovering the Parables**, (New York: Charles Scribner's Sons, 1966), p. 111.
23. M. J. Ollivier, **The Parables of Our Lord**, (The Richview Press, Clonskeaugh: Brown and Nolan Ltd., 1943), p. 228.
24. Bruce, op. cit., p. 316.
25. Wallace, op. cit., p. 104.
26. Ibid., p. 104.
27. Bruce, op. cit., p. 322.

The
Foolish
Farmer

10

THE PARABLE OF THE RICH FOOL
Luke 12:13-21

This parable sounds like the American dream —
building bigger and better barns. Anyone can find the
pot of gold at the end of the rainbow if only he has
enough grit, determination, ingenuity, and a little bit of
luck. Therefore, work hard, plan for the future and you
will be successful. We have all been raised on this kind of
advice.

By this same standard, the rich farmer in our parable
was a big success in the eyes of his neighbors and himself
because he was a builder of bigger and better barns. It
had been an especially good farm year. The rains had
been right. The fields had been warmed by sufficient
sunshine. The ground had been fertile. The bugs had been
few. The seeds had all sprouted into strong sturdy plants.
As a result the farmer had a bumper crop. In fact, it was
so abundant that it exceeded the capacity of all his
existing barns.

There the proud farmer stood surveying his bounty,
planning bigger and better barns, saying to himself,
"Lucky man! Lucky man!" Then it happened. Suddenly,
without warning, the voice of God thundered forth from
the heavens, "You fool!" This is really a great story.
Where in all the Bible could you find a greater dramatic
contrast? A proud achiever proclaiming to himself,
"Lucky man!" And the voice of God resounding from the
heavens, "You fool!"

The farmer now thought that he was going to sit back
and take it easy. His days of sweat and toil were over;
now he could retire and enjoy the fruits of his
abundance. Then suddenly his daydreams were

destroyed by the voice of God saying, "Fool! This very night you will have to give up your life." He was like a child whose balloon suddenly goes "pop." Or like the man who finds that his new oil well has suddenly gone dry. Or like the investor seeing the bottom dropping out of the stockmarket. One minute he was sure he had it made — he was a rich man with many possessions and great plans for spending them — the next minute he had nothing. He was suddenly stripped of everything by death.

Now our first reaction to this might be the tragic theme, "You Can't Take It With You." In the face of death all of our accomplishments and accumulations are cheap trinkets, worthless baubles, glass diamonds and fool's gold. However, there is more to this story than just the factual finality of death as the robber of all our riches. In order to discover this, we need to start at the beginning.

The Setting

Jesus had been assuring his disciples that if they were brought into court, the Holy Spirit would instruct them what to say. Now there was a man in the crowd who overheard these remarks and the words like "court," "lawsuits," "inheritance" were right down his alley. The ability to speak up in court was the very thing he had been seeking. So he came to Jesus for help, but unlike most who came to Jesus this man was refused and sent away. The first thing he did was to confront Jesus with a demand, "Teacher, tell my brother to divide with me the property our father left us." He did not, as most people, approach Christ with a question. Perhaps that is why Jesus rebuked him with such a stern statement, "Man, who gave me the right to judge or to divide the property between you two?"

Now it is true that such judgments were the responsibility of local lawyers and not teachers. But the man apparently felt that Jesus' popularity would give weight to his opinion in the community. Besides, what the young man had heard about Jesus indicated that this young rabbi played rather loosely with the Law. His opinions and interpretations were new and radical. He was concerned with fair treatment of the individual rather than strict adherence to the letter of the Law. So the man came to Jesus hoping for a special and exceptional ruling on the Law. But from what followed we know that Jesus saw in the request of the man not justice, but greed, for Jesus turns away from the man and speaks to the crowd, "Watch out and guard yourselves from all kinds of greed."

It is helpful to note that in the days of Jesus there were two important issues in domestic life — land and family loyalty. Land was scarce and it was essential that land be kept intact and not divided among the heirs. The farms were small and division would destroy their efficiency. So the law required that property in the form of land be given to the elder son.

The man who came to Jesus was undoubtedly the younger son who was thinking only of himself and not his father's efforts to maintain his precious land intact. Also, the young man had more than likely become angry with his older brother and had quarreled with him over the situation. Now he was exposing family matters in public, which was not a socially acceptable thing to do. Jesus was quick to see that the man's greed had driven him to a desire for an illegal dividing of the estate and a disgraceful division within the family. Jesus realized that what was needed was not a division, but a reunion between the two brothers. So Jesus uses the situation to save both the young man and us from falling into the disastrous tragedy of greed. He tells a parable that goes beyond greed and reveals an essential relationship between man and God.

208

A Good Fortune

Wallace presents this parable as a warning against
the wrong use of wealth. It shows "how riches and good
fortune in life tend to lead not to blessings but to
tragedy."[1] Wealth is dangerous when it leads to a false
sense of security, and to flattery that gives us a false
view of ourselves. But most of all, wealth is dangerous
because it tends to take over our lives and before we
know it, we are possessed by our possessions.

Two men once asked a holy man to adjudicate their
quarrel over the disputed ownership of a piece of land.
The holy man said that he would ask the land. He put his
ear to the ground and listened. After a few moments, he
stood up and facing the two men said, "The land says
that it belongs to neither of you, but you both belong to
it."

In the Old Testament, God is presented as rewarding
the righteous with earthly riches. Blessing was
equivalent to fruitful fields, abundant crops and growing
herds. The great men of the Old Testament like
Abraham, Moses, Saul and David, were prosperous men
of great earthly wealth. But in the New Testament the
poor and the humble people are blessed by God. It is
interesting that almost half the sayings of our Lord
concern the right use of riches. It appears that what was
considered a blessing in the Old Testament becomes a
threatening danger in the New. It is as if God discovers
that his people cannot handle great wealth. It makes
fools of them and deflects them from the main purposes
of life.

People take the blessing of great wealth and forget
from whom such blessings flow. It is as Luccock remarks
— the problem of failing to differentiate between
ownership and stewardship. We soon become more
fascinated with the gift than with the giver. We turn our
backs on God and become totally concerned with

accumulating more wealth. We never seem to be satisfied. As the old Roman proverb states, "Money is like sea-water; the more you drink the thirstier you are."

An old Quaker placed a sign on a choice plot of land, "This land will be given to the person who can prove to me he is a completely satisfied man." The Quaker barely made it back to his house before someone was at his door. "I saw your sign," the man said, "and I am truly a satisfied person. God has blessed me with a loving and faithful wife, obedient children, devoted friends, and a large and productive farm."

"Well," answered the Quaker, "if thou truly are a successful and satisfied man, then pray tell me, what dost thou want with this piece of land?" So God blesses us and the more he does, the more we want. That which we possess soon possesses us. Our blessings become our burdens that weigh us down to the unsatisfying task of acquiring more.

The Big "I"

Barclay[2] finds the dangers of riches in the fact that they blind us to everything except ourselves. He notes that in the parable the word "I" is used six times in only three verses. He began to think to himself, "I don't have a place to keep all my crops. What can I do? This is what I will do," he told himself, "I will tear down my barns and build bigger ones, where I will store my grain and all my other goods. Then I will say to myself, 'Lucky man.'"

Note the man says "all **my** crops" and "all **my** other goods." The man talks with himself when he should have been talking with God: "he told himself," "I will say to myself." We often tease our friends about talking to themselves. It is supposed to be a sign of slipping into a mental state of decay. But in the realm of religion, when a man begins to talk to himself, it is a sign that he has lost contact with God. He has become so wrapped up with himself that there is room for nothing else. As the little rhyme has it, "I gave a party and invited three, I, myself, and me."

George Bernard Shaw was once greeted by a hostess with the remark, "Make yourself at home, Mr. Shaw, and enjoy yourself." His famous remark was, "Madam, at **this** party that is the only one I can enjoy." This is the danger of riches, according to this parable; they create a pre-Copernican astronomy where everything revolves about your own little world.

End of the Age

Granskou[3] and Jeremias[4] focus in on the phrase, "This very night you will have to give up your life," and see the parable as a warning about the fragile quality of life. There is the finality of death which makes all our accumulations and accomplishments as nothing. The poor rich man in our parable learned too late that the abundance of one's life is not measured in terms of quantity — one's possessions — but in terms of quality — one's relationship to God and neighbor. The important thing is not how much one acquires, but how much one gives of himself to others. His foolishness was that he confused a full barn with a full life. He trusted and thought only of himself and his possessions and as the parable says, "... was not rich in God's sight."

The Collapse of Progress

Harvey is surprised to find Jesus in this parable being very philosophical. "Instead of pressing upon its hearers the demands of a new situation (like most of the parables), it appears to be simply an illustration of the age-old truth that man proposes and God disposes."[5] Harvey believes that the parable teaches that true riches are of another kind. Man should strive for treasures in heaven, not for earthly riches.

Glen calls his treatment of the parable "The Collapse of Progress." The man in the parable knew how to plan as well as work. "He looked forward to a time of leisurely retirement in which he could live off his accumulated resources and indulge himself in the sheer pleasure of living."[6] But suddenly his prosperous progress comes to an end. Where did the life of this man progress to? To an auction room where the accumulations of a lifetime were hammered off to the highest bidder. The parable states, "Then who will get all these things you have kept for yourself?" The inevitable answer is, "Strangers." There are no grateful friends or relatives to mourn him. This is the collapse of progress, when we fail to leave the world a better place than when we entered it, when we make no worthwhile contributions, offer no service, extend no generosity or kindness. When we spend our lives getting and not giving there is no progress, because we have shifted the wealth around but we have failed to make others richer for our having lived. When this is so we are rich but not in the sight of God. A rich life is one that enriches others.

Covetousness

Many scholars have focused in on the word **covetousness** when interpreting this parable. The Greek word used here literally means "the desire to have more." Hugh Martin[7] defines covetousness as the "folly that grasps at money under the impression that it means life." Herman Hanks[8] defines covetousness as the denial that all things belong to God. In the parable the rich man spoke of **my** crops, **my** barns, **my** grain, **my** goods, and **my** life. He stood on God's ground in the midst of God's harvest, brought forth by God's rain and God's sunshine and the fool said, "All this is mine!"

Covetousness is generally thought of in the Old

Testament as coveting the goods of your neighbor (the Tenth Commandment), but the parable seems to define covetousness as coveting our own property. Oesterley takes this a step further, pointing out that in this parable we see a man coveting for himself what belongs to God.[9]

The tragedy is that if it had been pointed out to the rich man that he was being covetous and greedy he would have denied it. He was only doing what any sensible man would do. He was preparing for the future. "After all, charity begins at home," we say. "And besides, I can't afford to be generous. When I am certain that my future is secure, then I can afford to think about others."

Hillyer Straton[10] catches this idea in the parable and sees it as a parable dealing with "The Sin of Security." He states that the desire for security has driven men to do almost anything for money. They go to such extremes because they are convinced that material abundance provides the only true security. The parable flatly denies this. It says that for true security — the security that a right relationship with God offers — no man can afford **not** to be generous.

Francis Xavier once said that men had confessed to him in the confessional every imaginable sin in the book, but that no one had ever confessed that he was covetous. Now one wonders why? Why is it that covetousness is so difficult for us to realize? I suppose it is because none of us really considers himself to be rich. We always want more and wanting more always makes us in our own estimation poor. And it is to this condition that our Lord speaks when he tells his parable. He warns us with a story which places in picture form an old rabbinic saying, "He who looks enviously on that which does not belong to him not only fails to obtain that which he seeks, but also loses that which he has."

Everything we have belongs to God; therefore, when we look upon that which we have as our own, belonging to us to do with what we please, we are being covetous. We do not have to look over the fence to our neighbor's possessions with an envious eye to be covetous; we just have to look at what we have and treat it as our own to become like the fool in the parable.

No Man Born a Fool

Fools are not born; they are made. We may be born sinners, but we are not born fools. Perhaps that is why Jesus was so hard on fools. They have no excuse. They bring this status on themselves.

At the beginning of the story we have the simple account of a rich man, industrious, hard-working and successful. Marcus Dods points out that there is no sin implied in the fact that the man was successful. He did not rob or steal his wealth from others, nor did he profit by another man's disaster.[11] Hugh Martin adds that money and success are not evil in themselves. "It is the love of it which the New Testament declares to be the root of all evil."[12] There is nothing in the teaching of our Lord that suggests that we should pretend to be indifferent to the decencies and pleasures of living which an adequate amount of money makes possible.

No, at the beginning of our story the man in our parable is no fool. He becomes a fool when he makes the wrong decision of what to do with his success. He asks himself the question, "What can I do with my abundance?" He had several options open to him. First, he could have **ignored** his bumper crops, neglecting them and letting them rot in the fields. Secondly, he could have sold them at a good price and like the prodigal gone for a fling in a far country and **wasted** his abundance in riotous living. But then not only would God have called him a fool, but his neighbors would have as well. Thirdly, he could have **shared** his good fortune.

Rather, he chose the fourth option. He would build

214

bigger barns in which to **store** his wealth. He could have helped and served many who were in need, but he chose to horde his money for himself. All about him were empty stomachs, empty homes, empty lives crying out to be filled, but he built bigger barns and filled them up for himself. And at the very moment that he made that decision he became the fool.

It should also be added that his question was wrong. He asked, "What shall I do?" He should have asked, "Lord what would you have me do with this abundance?" The real issue presented here is not the question of how much do we have, but how can we use what we have? And this applies to our talents, our time and our very lives as well as our money. We are either wise stewards who serve the Lord and our neighbor, or fools who serve only ourselves.

Fool

As we have already pointed out, most of us do not consider ourselves to be rich. We pride ourselves on a middle class status that protects us from the degradation of being poor and the condemnation of being rich. We occupy the safe middle ground in between.

However, the key word in the parable is "fool," not "rich." This is not a story of the foolishness of being rich, but how quickly riches can make a fool out of us. But it is equally true that a poor man can become a fool because of his poverty. Perhaps not as often, but the danger is still there, because foolishness is not equated in the parable with possessing riches. If you were to take a stick and stir up this story you would discover that more than one fool would break loose from the social strata and float to the surface. The servants who worked for this man — many of them — would have gladly killed him if they thought there was a chance of getting their hands on some of his wealth. Many merchants who were his friends would have willingly cheated him out of his wealth if they thought they could have gotten away with it. It was the lack of opportunity that covered their covetousness. And undoubtedly most of his neighbors envied his success. They would have traded places with the rich farmer at the drop of a hat. And they would have built barns just as big to horde the wealth for themselves. It was their lack of ability and ambition in a competitive economy that covered their covetousness. So you see, there is more than one fool in this tale if the full truth were known. In fact, there is enough room in this story for every fool who listens to it.

Filas points out that "the expression, 'Thou, fool,' meant much more to the Jewish mind than a mere term of contempt."[13] The word 'fool' used here is not used as we commonly understand the word. We casually say to each other, "Don't be foolish," or "Don't make a fool of yourself." And when we do, we mean a kind of comic jester that once amused the royalty at court. This is not a complimentary thing to say, but at the same time it is not a severe condemnation.

In the scripture, however, the word 'fool' is quite different in meaning. It is seldom used and when it does appear it is used with great caution. The word 'fool' is really a severe indictment against a person.

Jesus regards with great seriousness the irresponsible use of the word 'fool.' In the Sermon on the Mount he says, "Whoever says, 'You fool,' shall be liable to the hell of fire." The meaning of the word 'fool' is defined in the Psalms where it states, "The fool says in his heart there is no God." The word, therefore, means a person who does not blatantly deny God but is indifferent to him. It is as some theologians have pointed out "a practical atheism," which is the most damaging state to be in so far as belief in God is concerned.

The intellectual atheist is concerned about the issue of God. He has thought the matter through and has

216

serious convictions based upon what are to him sound reasons. He does not treat the reality of God lightly, but his thought leads him to the belief that there is no God. The practical atheist, on the other hand, is not at all concerned about the issue of the reality of God. He couldn't care less. He has given no serious thought to it whatsoever. He just doesn't think about God at all and therefore lives as if there is no God.

In many ways this is the exact opposite of faith — not doubt, but indifference. Therefore, it is more dangerous than doubt and more self-damning. Lincoln once said that "I don't care if you agree or disagree with me so long as you don't ignore me." The intellectual atheist has not ignored God; he has taken him quite seriously but he has dismissed the existence of God as an unreasonable option. The practical atheist, on the other hand, ignores God. And this is the most insulting thing man can do to God.

In His Heart

This little phrase is also important. The heart is the center of personality. It is the point of origin of all our motivations, actions, thoughts and emotions. If there is indifference in the heart, then all we do or think proceeds from an attitude and an assumption that leaves God entirely out of the picture. This is pure secularism.

So the real issue of the parable is not riches, but playing the fool — being a person who says in his heart, "There is no God." The fool is blind to God and deaf. True, in this story it is his riches that have blinded and deafened him, but anything that blinds and deafens us to God and our need for him makes us fools. When we trust in sound insurance programs, large bank accounts, blue chip stock, diet and regular exercise, health care plans, annual medical check-ups, preventative shots, good family relations and then neglect God — we are still fools with no future. No matter how wise we are in the ways of the world, death will ultimately make fools of us all. For God and God alone makes all of our efforts to gain more out of life worthwhile and meaningful — for God alone can give us a life that is victorious over death.

When you come right down to it, this parable says to us that as Christians the sign of the abundant life is not bumper crops and full barns, but a rugged cross and an empty tomb. The full barns of earthly accomplishments are easily taken from us, but through the cross and the empty tomb our Lord and Savior gives us the gift of a life that shall never die!

Notes

1. Ronald S. Wallace, **Many Things in Parables**, (New York: Harper and Brothers, 1955), pp. 145-146.
2. William Barclay, **The Gospel of Luke**, (Philadelphis: Westminster Press, 1956), p. 168.
3. David M. Granskou, **Preaching on the Parables**, (Philadelphia: Fortress Press, 1972), p. 84.
4. Joachim Jeremias, **Rediscovering the Parables**, (New York: Scribner and Sons, 1966), p. 77.
5. A. E. Harvey, **Companion to the New Testament**, (Oxford: Oxford University Press, 1971), p. 258.
6. J. Stanley Glen, **The Parables of Conflict in Luke**, (Philadelphia: Westminster Press, 1962), p. 78.
7. Hugh Martin, **The Parables of the Gospel and Their Meaning**, London: SCM, 1937), p. 140.
8. Herman C. Hanko, **The Mysteries of the Kingdom**, (Grand Rapids: Reformed Free Publishing Assn., 1975), p. 94.
9. W.O.E. Oesterley. **The Gospel Parables in the Light of Their Jewish Background**, (London: SPCK, 1936), p. 173.
10. Hillyer Hawthorne Straton, **A Guide to the Parables**, (Grand Rapids: Eerdmans, 1959), p. 83.
11. Marcus Dods, **The Parables of Our Lord**, (New York: Fleming H. Revell), p. 282.
12. Hugh Martin, op. cit., p. 140.
13. Francis L. Filas, **The Parables of Jesus**, (New York: Macmillan, 1959), p. 52.

The
Happy
Household

11

THE PARABLE OF THE WATCHFUL SERVANTS
Luke 12:32-40

A young man was speeding down the road when he saw a train and decided to race it to the crossing. It ended up a tie and the young man lost. His family decided to sue the railroad for there should have been a watchman on duty at this dangerous crossing. The railroad officials called in the man assigned to the place where the accident happened. They asked him if he were there, if he were awake, and if he attempted to warn the approaching motorist that a train was coming. The watchman assured them that he was on the job. He was awake and he went out and waved his lantern but the young driver paid no attention to it.

The case was brought to trial. Under severe cross-examination on the witness stand, the watchman stuck to his story. After the trial was over, the head of the railroad called the watchman into his office and told him how pleased the company was to have such a dependable employee. "I was afraid," the president said, "that you might back down on your story and admit you fell asleep." "No," the watchman replied, "I was awake and on the job. But you know, I was afraid, too — I was afraid one of them smart lawyers was going to ask me if my lantern was lit."

Now it makes a great deal of difference whether or not a lantern is lit. Today, within the church there is a great deal of activity, but much of it is simply the waving of unlighted lanterns. There is a lack of total involvement and commitment. We do the work but not very thoroughly. We do just enough to get by. We do not take the responsibility of Christian service and stewardship seriously enough.

To such a situation Jesus tells the story of the watchful servants. It is a story stressing the need for total preparation. Like the watchman in our story, we are to be on the job, awake with lanterns lit. He says, "Let your loins be girded." That means be ready for action. In the days of our Lord, men wore long, flowing robes and when there was work to be done they would gather up their robes and fasten them with a girdle so that they wouldn't be in the way. From this ancient expression, "Gird up your loins," we get the modern expression, "Pull yourself together." And that is literally what Jesus was saying. "Be alert, be ready for action, be altogether alert."

Then Jesus adds, "have your lamps burning," which is another common expression of his day meaning vigorous vigilance and total watchfulness. Now this theme of complete preparedness occurs all through the gospels. Again and again the message of our Lord to his followers is readiness, preparedness, watchfulness. Be prepared for a sudden unexpected happening.

Now this parable is seldom dealt with in books on the parables. The scholars who do treat it fail to agree as to the exact intent of our Lord when he told the story originally. A great deal depends on the original audience. To whom did Jesus direct this parable? There are several possibilities. First, Christ could have had in mind the fall of Jerusalem. Jeremias[1] considers this a strong possibility and states that it was originally addressed to the scribes whom Granskou describes as the "watch dogs of Israel."[2] If this were the case, Jesus was challenging the scribes to see if they were sufficiently prepared for the calamity which was soon to come to the whole nation of Israel.

A second possibility is that Jesus was speaking to the disciples. He knew that his message and mission was going to stir up trouble and create a crisis. He was also well aware that his claims would be contested by the people in power and that he would create strong enemies. It was a dangerous and explosive situation and this meant that vigilance and alertness would be demanded of all those who followed him.

A third possibility is that our Lord was addressing this to everyone who heard him. It was a warning of the imminent but still unpredictable hour of general judgment which was to come upon the whole world. Harvey, however, comments that Luke in the chapter in which this parable occurs says very little about the future. "It looks as if Luke deliberately shifted the emphasis of this teaching from the prediction of future woes and rewards to the inculcation of the right attitude in the present."[3]

Dodd believes the original intent and meaning of this parable is impossible to establish. However, he speculates that it could have been used to teach the general lesson, "Be alert and prepared for any development in this critical situation."[4] On the other hand, Dodd is convinced that whatever the original intent of our Lord when he told this parable, there is little doubt that the early Church used the parable to teach Christians that they should be alert and constantly prepared for the Last Day, the Second Coming of Christ, and the Final Judgment.[5]

Jeremias comes to the same conclusion. He sees this parable as related to Mark's parable of the Doorkeeper (Mark 13:33-37). Jeremias believes that Luke takes the doorkeeper in Mark and expands this figure into a whole staff of servants who are to watch so that the parable could be applied to the whole Christian community and not just to a few leaders whose special responsibility it was to be alert to that day when Jesus would return again in glory.

Jeremias is struck by the fact that the watchful servants are rewarded for their watchfulness. The master girds himself and serves his servants. "No earthly master behaves like that," states Jeremias, "but Jesus has done so (Luke 22:27; John 13:4-5) and he will do so again on his return."[6] Charles Smith is also impressed with this detail of the story and sees the "girding" as referring to the "humility of Christ and suggests the foot-washing scene in John 13:1-16."[7]

Filas goes one step further and completely allegorizes the parable. He concludes, "But the master is evidently Jesus himself, who hints at the reward he as God has prepared for his faithful servants."[8] Smith, on the other hand, denounces an allegorical interpretation and settles for a lesson of promise as the meaning of the parable. The promise is, "Those who are found girded ready for service will **receive** that which they were prepared to **offer**."[9]

The weight of evidence from the scholars is that the parable is a general warning to be watchful, for this time (any time) is a time of crisis for the disciples, for Jesus and for the nation of Israel. Or as Eta Linnemann puts it, the parable is a "general exhortation to watchfulness."

The Parable of the Happy Household

When the parable is looked at from the point of view of Narrative Theology, simply as a story, some interesting insights emerge. It is really the story about a happy master who has happy servants and they all live together in a happy household.

The story begins with a rich man who has many servants. In contrast with the Parable of the Rich Fool which immediately precedes it, this is the story of a rich man who knew what to do with his wealth. He apparently shared it with his servants.

The master is invited to a wedding feast. His servants, of course, were not invited. They had to stay at home and miss all the fun and festivities. But they wait for their master to come home with great excitement because they know their master is a good man and he will share with them the enjoyment of the banquet's festivities.

When he comes home from the party, they eagerly rush to open the door to greet him. They can hardly wait until he knocks to open the door. All the lamps are lighted and everything is prepared as if a party is about to happen. As soon as the master comes in the door, that is exactly what happens. The parable states that the master "girds himself." Today that would mean he put on an apron and had all the servants sit down at the table to be served by him.

To understand what is happening in this parable, we need to know that it was a custom in the days of our Lord that when a great banquet was given, not only the invited guests but the whole community shared in the festivities. The food that was left over could not be stored, for there were no means of preserving freshly-cooked food in that hot climate. Even a king's palace had no refrigerator. So the left-over food was given to the servants and the other people in the village so that none would be wasted. It was first given to the women of the family, then to the children, then to the servants and neighbors so that the food filtered out into the whole village and everybody, even the lowest of the slaves, would get at least a taste of the banquet fare.

In the parable Jesus told, the master undoubtedly thought of his servants at home. He knew that they would enjoy the marvelous treats that covered the table. So after the party was over, he gathered all he could carry and left the party loaded down with left-over goodies. Today we would say that he filled a "doggy bag" for those at home.

Now his servants must have experienced this before, and that is why they waited for him with such eager anticipation. They knew that when their master came home there would be treats for them all. And that is exactly what happened. He walked in the door loaded down with goodies.

Now so far in the story, the original listeners of the parable must have thought to themselves, this master was a very good man to treat his servants so kindly and to remember them and include them in on the festivities of the banquet. But then a surprise entered into the story. The master didn't just give the servants their treats as one would pass out scraps to unfortunates, but he put on an apron and became a servant host. He sat his servants down to the table and made of them his guests. "Amazing," the listeners to the story must have said. "What an amazingly **good** man this master is!"

The only conclusion that could have been drawn from this story in the days of our Lord is that this certainly was a picture of a happy household. The master loved the servants, and the servants loved the master. The servants were good to the master and the master was unusually good to his servants. "I certainly would like to be a member of that happy household," the original hearers must have said.

Jesus told this parable to describe the relationship that should exist between God and his people. The church should be a happy household because we have such a good and loving God. God is a God who willingly becomes a servant to assure that we become happy guests.

Luke places this parable in a setting where Jesus is talking to his disciples. He is telling them not to worry about the food they need to stay alive or about the clothes they need for their bodies. They are to trust in God. Jesus states in verse twenty-seven just before this parable, "Look how the wild flowers grow: they don't work or make clothes for themselves. But I tell you that not even Solomon, as rich as he was, had clothes as beautiful as one of these flowers." Jesus is describing a happy kingdom where all needs are met by a loving God.

Our lesson opens with the words, "Do not be afraid, little flock! For your Father is pleased to give you the Kingdom." Be happy, Jesus is saying. And after the parable, in a discussion with Peter, our Lord says (Verse 43), "How happy is that servant if his master finds him doing this when he comes home." Jesus is describing a happy Kingdom where a happy God provides for his happy servants.

When Jesus first told this parable, this was a strange description of the Kingdom and of God. For his Jewish listeners, God was the holy God of the temple who dwelt behind a veil of secrecy in total darkness. Outside in the temple courtyards, priests performed complex rituals and offered sacrifices without blemish to appease and please an austere God. No one dared enter his presence except the high priest and then only once a year on the day of Atonement. All through the Old Testament, God was so holy and separated away from man and his daily tasks that even the name of God was too holy to mention. The rabbis and the Pharisees taught that God was a severe judge and they presented his will in a complex system of many laws that must be obeyed to the letter. There was no warmth here, no happiness, only fear.

Then Jesus came with a revolutionary teaching concerning God. He called him Father, or Papa to be more exact. He presented him as a forgiving and loving father, a God of mercy and grace. The big word in Jesus' religious vocabulary was not **holy** but **happy.** When he preached the Sermon on the Mount and described what it would be like to be a member of the Kingdom of God, he began each Beatitude with 'happy': "Happy are the poor in spirit, Happy are the meek, Happy are the merciful, Happy are the pure in heart." Happy, happy, happy! Jesus literally introduces the word 'happy' into the realm of divine revelation.

Therefore, when he wants to talk about his coming again, he tells a parable about a happy household, the story about a master and his servants who have a party when the master returns to them. This is an amazing teaching. It is really unbelievable — such a radical religious notion that religion should make people happy. But that is exactly what Jesus is saying as he tells this parable. The children of the true God are a happy household.

Now the tragedy is that today, after two thousand years, so few of us proclaim and practice this happy holiness. In our lives we fail to reflect the happiness that should mark our lives and testify to the fact that we have a loving father for a God. Rather, we think of religion as a burden of things we must do and must not do which produces a faith marked more by fear than celebration. Jesus says to us, "Fear not, little flock, for it is your father's good pleasure to give you the Kingdom." Note! Not God's duty, or his task, or his responsibility, but his **good pleasure.** In other words, God is happy to do it, for doing it makes him happy, and if it doesn't make us happy, something is radically wrong. For true holiness is happiness.

What a marvelous note on which to end our study of the parables. In each we have seen the triumph of divine grace. In each we have seen a loving and forgiving father God who wants more than anything else to give us everything we need. He is a God of generosity and grace. With such a gospel how can we fail to be happy?

Notes

1. Joachim Jeremias, **Rediscovering the Parables,** (New York: Charles Scribner's Sons, 1966), p. 43.
2. David M. Granskou, **Preaching on the Parables,** (Philadelphia: Fortress Press, 1972), p. 116.
3. A. E. Harvey, **Companion to the New Testament,** (Oxford: Oxford University Press, 1971), p. 258.
4. Charles Dodd, **The Parables of the Kingdom**, (London: Nisbet and Co., rev. ed., 1961), p. 165.
5. Ibid., p. 162.
6. Jeremias, op. cit., p. 41.
7. Charles W. F. Smith, **The Jesus of the Parables,** (Philadelphia: United Church Press, 1971), p. 177.
8. Francis L. Filas, **The Parables of Jesus,** (New York: Macmillan, 1959), p. 157.
9. Smith, op. cit., p. 177.
10. Eta Linnemann, **Jesus of the Parables,** (New York: Harper and Row, 1946), p. 135.